Applying Entrepreneurship
to the Arts

Applying Entrepreneurship to the Arts

How Artists, Creatives, and Performers
Can Use Startup Principles to Build
Careers and Generate Income

Paula Landry

Routledge
Taylor & Francis Group

A PRODUCTIVITY PRESS BOOK

First published 2022
by Routledge
605 Third Avenue, New York, NY 10158

and by Routledge
4 Park Square, Milton Park, Abingdon, Oxon, OX14 4RN

Routledge is an imprint of the Taylor & Francis Group, an informa business

ISBN: 9781032125602 (hbk)
ISBN: 9781032125572 (pbk)
ISBN: 9781003225140 (ebk)

DOI: 10.4324/9781003225140

Typeset in Garamond
by Deanta Global Publishing Services, Chennai, India

Contents

Preface

You're at a specific place in time, space, and life. The entrepreneurial journey may deepen your existing work or help you find something new. Are you seeking a side hustle, lifestyle business, or company that could be sold? While it's great to understand that when you start out, that may be a process of discovery (Figure P.1).

Entrepreneurship discovery includes:

- Planning
- Time to build and test
- The process of creating with constraints
- Bravery to share with awareness
- Committing to generating results with your launch
- Time allocated to manage your venture and analyze results

At every phase of the process, your skills, abilities, experience, knowledge, training, and natural gifts are included. Welcomed. Your past successes in every field and occasion are brought into the process, to inform this work. The shape of our journey together covers the traditional processes in business – ideation, testing, marketing, prototyping, legal, financial, management, and administrative tasks – but they are shaped for this moment and your creative approach. This work is not exclusive of your talents; it's inclusive. The shape of the process is cyclical; each new offering that you make and sell deepens your understanding of the next. And the next … The world will never implore you to make and share your creativity, but we need it so much. We will appreciate your vision once we can share in it.

Startups that flourish make more money than they spend. They sell something customers want. You must generate or find something to sell.

Getting Started

Figure P.1   By DeAngela Napier and Paula Landry.

Entrepreneurship is typically focused on making money, but it's understood that profits aren't the same thing as success. Success is fluid, and you need to define that for yourself, as well as what creative fulfillment means to you.

Side by side with profitability, positivity is important throughout this journey. For artistic people, emotional management adds rocket fuel to results. Allow yourself, invite yourself, and engage yourself in a positive and optimistic mindset as you proceed. Manage your feelings and energy to utilize time and money easily, and with flow.

Feel good. Have fun. Share your creativity with a world that needs it so much. Make money.

You can do this!

Paula Landry

Acknowledgments

Thank you to everyone who supported me in this endeavor. I appreciate your help. All the good vibes, interviews, chats, and inspiration – from all the creative people I know. Huge thank you to the Taylor & Francis team and the Routledge family. I would like to express waves of gratitude to my fantastic editor Michael Sinocchi, for all of this guidance and inspiration in our collaboration, as well as my wonderful editorial assistant Samantha Dalton for her attention to file wrangling, details, and help with logistics. Shout-out and warm thank you to Katherine Kadian for linking this book with Michael Sinocchi and Productivity Press!

I would like to thank my amazing husband Rick Mowat for his encouragement, patience, computer savvy, and assistance. I couldn't have done this without the inspiration delivered by the memory of my parents, both outstanding entrepreneurs, Irene Landry and Robert Landry; may they rest in peace. Love and recognition to my family who sustain me in all creative endeavors, Donna Landry, Claudia, Doug, Cherie, Lisa, Sindi, Pam, Wayne, Melissa, Tyler, Zander, Angela, all my cousins, my aunts, and my uncle. Wonderful cheerleaders! Salutations and appreciation for Barb Lindsay and Bruce Todesco, as well as Sharon Lindsay, thank you so much for your encouragement. Big shout-out to Thanhha Lai and An Lai for their cheerleading throughout this process.

Tremendous gratitude to creative graphics guru, DeAngela Napier. Thank you so much for your artistry and collaboration here.

I would like to warmly thank the brilliant creative entrepreneurs who spoke to me and shared their creative gifts in service of this work empowering creatives, such as musician Bryan Steele; filmmaker and mentor Steve Greenwald; photographer Charles Chessler; filmmakers Cidney Hue and Lauren Sowa, the co-presidents of PANO/NYC Women Filmmakers;

content creator Toni D'Antonio from Shake the Tree Productions; incomparable filmmaker and businesswoman Eve Honthaner; musician and activist Maya Azucena.

To all the artists, creators, performers, entertainers out there who make, create, and share their creativity with the world – you are an inspiration to me every day!

Author

Paula Landry, MBA, is an author and award-winning writer/producer who works in film, television, and media entrepreneurship. Her clients include brands, creatives, and companies, big and small. As a creator, her purpose is to reduce loneliness, connect with people through stories and ideas, and link artists with entrepreneurial tools and clients with increased revenue and visibility. She is the author of *Scheduling and Budgeting Your Film: A Panic – Free Guide*, 2nd ed. (Taylor & Francis) and co-author with Stephen Greenwald of *The Business of Film, A Practical Guide*, 3rd ed. (Taylor & Francis).

Landry consults on corporate creativity, creating creative entrepreneurship programs, VR film project development, educational media curriculums and initiatives for corporations, non-profits, as well as movie and media education for diverse populations.

Clients include Fortune 500 companies, creative entrepreneurs, and non-profits, from Forbes, Deutsche Bank, Christie's, Pearson Television, Entertainment Weekly, The Game Show Channel, Panasonic, Fit TV to The Actors Fund, Mission Society, Smile Train, and individual media makers. Her films have debuted at Sundance, Chelsea Film Festival, and CineVegas, winning awards from the Best Actors Film Fest, Columbia Pictures Screen Gems, Time Warner Showtime Audience Award, and WorldFest Houston Film Festival; her writing has won the Lugnut Award, 2nd Round at Austin Film Festival, and has been a semi-finalist at Made in NY Writer's Room. Ms. Landry is a member of Disney's Creative Talent Development & Inclusion program.

She generates hope and strategies with her collaborators, no matter what field. Services she offers to clients include budgets, business plans, financing strategies, as well as fundraising decks for clients in filmmaking, commercials, and social media. Recent projects include two Christmas movies, three episodic television projects, the comedic Irish crime thriller *Last Pint*, developing Warren Adler's (*War of the Roses*) play *Dead in the Water* for the screen, and the Stage to Screen – Script Contest, seeking to develop projects for both stage and on-screen.

She joyfully serves as a volunteer board member for the non-profit organization New York City Women Filmmakers. Additionally, she enjoys working as a creative coach, teaching entrepreneurship and mentoring writers and filmmakers, and seeks to learn all the time! As a consultant, Ms. Landry conducts financial library valuations for film, theater, literary, and television properties in association with G&H Media.

She teaches media to graduate students in New York City, also conducting seminars on media and entrepreneurship worldwide: Cuba, Haifa, Europe, and more.

Chapter 1

Plan

To move ahead – in almost any creative area, planning is key. There can be value in creating without a specific aim; however, once you have an entrepreneurial mindset, planning will get you there faster.

What is planning?

- Selecting a goal
- Organizing and preparing your efforts before proceeding
- The best way to save time, money, and energy
- Utilizing simple frameworks to achieve desired results

An entrepreneurial plan includes where you want to go, why you're heading there. It helps focus your work. Your plan may include the actions, mindset, and strategy to start and successfully generate a certain amount of income. Planning incorporates your entire self. It employs your creative skills and other abilities. This begins with articulating that vision.

No matter whether your ultimate plan includes a new model of success, or ultimately working for yourself, it's important to understand that and know where you are now. Planning, goal setting, and dreaming go together because you can chase something only to find you were chasing the wrong thing. The purpose of this is customizable, based on what you seek.

Planning articulates something you want to change and the direction. Goal setting illustrates the steps in that direction. Dreaming motivates both. Vision adds emotion and value throughout.

DOI: 10.4324/9781003225140-1

Once you generate a plan with goals, you may very well change them. That's okay. Planning is a means of uniting your energy and ideas to go in a specific direction. No plan at all often means going in circles or doing nothing. Imagining where you want to go gives you a direction to move toward the goal. Deciding to plan will get you moving. Activating your plan offers clear actions to take.

Here's what planning should do:

- Add direction to your work
- Offer motivation as you make progress
- Give you a way to measure your progress
- Get you excited
- Activate you to do

Here's what planning shouldn't do:

- Paralyze you with information overload
- Make you feel guilty
- Put negative pressure on you
- Compare yourself unfavorably to others
- If any of these things happen – stop. Start doing the next right thing

What planning effectively does is help you choose. Decisions are simpler. You can do almost anything but not everything, so by eliminating time-wasters, entrepreneurs can use laser-like focus with their time and energy. Effective ways to plan should make you feel excited and happy about what you're doing, as well as propel you forward. To do that, it's important to look at your goals and your skills (primary and secondary) that you can employ with daydreaming exercises to move forward with your startup. The aim is to utilize your unique talents, skills, and artistic abilities and discover your profitable business. By planning what you want, dream to open up and expand the possibilities of those ideas to find the right business ideas for you that harness your unique abilities and purpose. Initially, your plan can consist of putting appointments on your calendar to do the entrepreneurial work.

Creative people have many of the same problems everyone else does, but some are more prevalent. Common issues are becoming overwhelmed, feeling self-doubt, and losing track of time.

If you are experiencing overwhelm. Pause. Gather yourself, and then just do the next action. You may recognize this with feelings of panic and thoughts swirling in a loop. If that happens, stop. Breathe. Acknowledge the feelings. Exhale forcefully to slow your heartbeat, stretch, and step away for a moment if you need to. Then say, now I'm doing the next right thing and start acting, doing, and working as if you knew what you should be doing. One thing at a time.

If you have the feeling of self-doubt, recall a vivid memory of when you succeeded and felt great. That success could be in any arena. Enjoy and savor the sensations of that occasion. You CAN do it. Practice positive self-talk and repeat it, constantly. Say the phrases out loud in a convincing tone or record a positive affirmation. You have skills and talents that you carry around all the time, and you need to channel that outlook during this process. Activate your superpowers by visualizing a moment in your past when you did something great. Carry that feeling and mindset with you.

If you're someone who often loses track of time (which can be great and a curse depending on what's going on), set timers. Loud timers. Use your phone, Internet timer, or watch, and set them every time you start something. Stay aware of boredom and distractibility, schedule yourself for success to combat these (Figure 1.1).

What are the tools for planning? It depends on whether you enjoy digital tools or real-world tools. Use an app for your mobile phone; specific project management software, paper, and pen, whatever is helpful for you. Initially the plan should include purpose, passion, skills, talents, why you want to do this and when, where, and how you'll work on it.

Daydreaming with Purpose

Daydreaming is the practice of visually creating a reality in your mind's eye that you can then move toward by your actions, goals, purpose, intention, partnerships, and plans. For many of us, this comes naturally, and we do it without thinking, however, we can harness the process of dreaming to inform our creativity and goals. To imagine something is the first step in producing anything, from an invention to a business or song.

By daydreaming about starting the kind of business that would be enjoyable, profitable, utilizes your skills, and also makes you feel good; your complete mind helps you create what you're imagining.

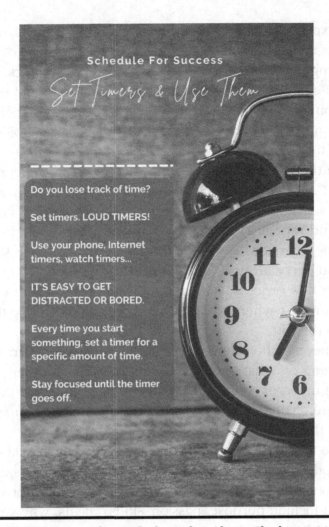

Figure 1.1 Schedule success. Photo Black Analog Alarm Clock at 7:01 by Aphiwat Chuangchoem from Pexels, CC0.

When you daydream, your mind cycles through different modes of thinking, and during this time, the analytic and empathetic parts of your brain tend to turn each other off. The very nature of this is the cessation of directed thinking. Fantasizing, like meditation, is good for you, and it isn't necessary to direct what you're dreaming about, it's letting the mind wander and play. Whether you call this dreaming, manifesting, meditation, or hypnotherapy, the entire point is to allow your conscious mind and subconscious mind to cooperate in your planning. You do not actively pursue a particular state, and if thoughts and emotions intrude, you let them pass in an effortless way.

Manifesting is the practice of thinking thoughts with the purpose of making them real, and the term has become very popular. With fans and critics alike, creative visualization is where planning begins, whether you call it manifestation or meditation. The idea is that you're open to creating your dreams – and that's the key. Once you are clear on your dreams and goals, then act on them.

Meditation is an age-old practice of many cultures. Close your eyes, become aware of your breathing, and let your mind go.

Depending on whether you respond to visual, auditory, or textual cues, there are a number of ways to help you move toward proactive daydreaming meditation and visualization.

Here are some tools to help propel you into dreaming:

Tools

- Music or meditative tones
- A startup journal and pen, or computer files for all your activities
- Timer: Meditation apps such as Plum Village, Insight Timer, and Headspace, or on your watch, the Internet, or egg timer

Exercises

The point is to collect a list of your skills, from the organic and innate to those cultivated over time. For a warm-up, with pen and paper, start drawing circles, over and over. Keeping the pen connected to the paper is a hand motion that promotes creativity (Figure 1.2).

Dream Openers: Give yourself permission to daydream and enjoy the process. Set a timer for 3–10 minutes. Here's a way into fruitful dreaming:

- If you like, play relaxing music
- Notice your breath, relax your body
- Start Happy to Neutral – What gets you in a good to neutral mood? Start there
- Visual – Imagine a positive visual cue
- Auditory – Imagine wonderful sound to open a dream state
- Other senses may serve as a gateway into the dream state

Dream Flow:

- Make fluid circles with your hands in the air for a few minutes
- Sit quietly, relax, or close your eyes
- Breathe effortlessly

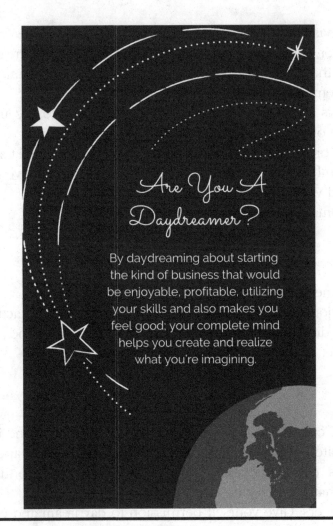

Figure 1.2   Dreaming by DeAngela Napier and Paula Landry.

- Let whatever you want drift into your mind
- When the timer goes off, begin your skills list

After Dreaming: Create Your Skills List.

   The following is an exercise to do *after* you have spent some time daydreaming or meditating. Once you are done, your mental state should be open. Answer the following questions that are relevant to you. Don't think too hard about these, just answer and move on.

- What are you naturally good at?
- The last time you were in a state of flow, what were you doing?
- What activities excite you?

- What are your primary skills?
- Which inter-related secondary skills are you often praised for?
- What work or career experience have you gathered?
- What does everyone ask you for help with?
- What skills would you enjoy sharing with others?
- Could any of these skills be sold as something tangible, like a good or product?
- Could any of these skills be sold as a service?
- Could any of these skills be sold as an experience?

Keep this list for later.

From this exercise, themes may emerge to guide you in your entrepreneurial journey, and you should jot them down where you'll see them often. Use these to identify your first goals to move toward.

TIP: Just like getting into a fitness habit, if you want to enhance your innovative powers, the first step is to practice daydreaming. Add daydreaming into your schedule as you would with any other practice, set aside a convenient moment to build this habit, when you wake, just before sleep, or during some habitual activity like a commute, coffee break, or walk.

Goal Setting

Once you've invited your subconscious mind to let your conscious mind know what you really want to do, it is time to identify your goals. Many creative artists, performers, and entertainers have many goals. The point is to hone in on the main ones that will move you forward.

Defining Your Goals

Discovering and articulating your goals start with the basics. You may want to work for yourself, make more money in a side-hustle, or explore something new that's fun and utilizes your creativity. Perhaps collaboration or self-direction is the most important, all of that is up to you. It may take some time; give yourself a few days but no more than a week to define your goals. Sometimes you have to look in unlikely places and the space around your goals. Develop the meaning of your goals by defining them to make sure they are motivating your work and purpose and pointing your efforts in the right direction. Writing down your goals will help to achieve them.

Exercise

Grab your startup journal. Spend a moment daydreaming – what would your perfect working day look like? Briefly describe the things that excite you, whether that's flexible scheduling, interesting partnerships, or a creative challenge. Then answer the following:

■ What do you want to achieve within the next 3 months to a year with your venture?
■ What are three to five of your primary entrepreneurial goals relating to that?
■ Which is the most exciting goal for you?

Now you have some goals to play with. Pick a goal on the exciting side. Add a framework of details. For example, "I want to be more successful this year" is a great start but needs specificity. Think about the people who inspire you. Borrow from them. Ask yourself what that person would do in your shoes. One way of achieving your goals is to model behaviors of others to get motivated, inspired, and specific with yourself (Figure 1.3).

Modeling: Who inspires you? Are they an example that you can follow to fulfill your startup aspirations? Select a heroine or inspirational figure in your field as an example.

Modeling a person you admire (or company, but it's better if you chose an actual person) is a way for you to copy the behaviors, mindsets, and patterns of excellence you see in another. Is there a person who comes to mind right away? It's best to select one or two entrepreneurs or creative business people who resonate with your values, and if possible, are working in or around your field. Learn what you can about them and follow their behavior. Learning how others have achieved their goals is one way to stay motivated, and define your goals more specifically.

Whether you select a ballerina, chef, dancer, stylist, painter, or athlete, the point is to channel what is working for them. Adopt those attitudes and behaviors. This doesn't have to be literal; it's rather finding a great example, and it can be someone you know, who inspires you, and makes you want to do your best. When you get down or feel discouraged, think about what that person might do in your shoes, and use that for encouragement. (An excellent source for this research that's already done is the Tim Ferriss book, *Tools of Titans*, with summaries of some remarkable individuals.)

Exercise: Make a list of the obvious startup models in your field who are doing what you want to be doing, and profitably. How are they generating

Goal Setting

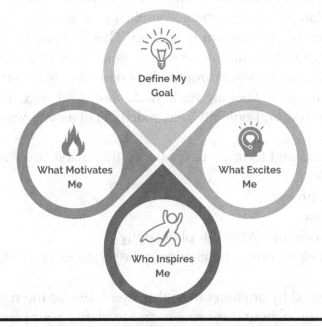

Figure 1.3　Goal Setting by DeAngela Napier and Paula Landry.

profits by what they sell? Ask yourself if it's possible and realistic that you can do something similar. What would be the very first step? These may be peers or colleagues who have attained a level of expertise you aspire to or established companies.

- Take a few minutes and research your potential models, finding everything out about them that you can. Now you have models for excellence
- Make a list of what they sell that you admire and the traits that could help you succeed in your plans
- Look at their website, services, and products; subscribe to their newsletter; and follow their socials
- Borrow their example in your journey

Now that you have thought about your inspirations and studied high achievers, it's time to write your short business story (or speak it aloud into a recorder). The following exercise allows you a gateway to imagine you're already through your journey, reflecting back. Sometimes to look forward we must first look back to tap into our motivation. If you are familiar with Wikipedia, it is the Internet encyclopedia. Imagine many years in the future you're looking back at all that you've accomplished. By envisioning great end results (never mind all the details), you construct a big picture view of how you can plan for success and accomplish your goals.

Optional Exercise: Brainstorm your Wiki. This is an exercise that's meant to be done without criticism, in one sitting, quickly. Read a Wikipedia profile of a person you admire. Skim through their narrative. Now, project yourself into a successful future. Looking back, draft your Wiki page. Don't think too hard. Use an outline and only fill in as much detail as you want.

1. Your interests and formative experience that made you want to begin your startup
2. First breakthrough
3. Next success
4. Stylistic trademarks AND/OR philosophy
5. How you helped others by changing the world or philanthropic work

Were you surprised by anything from this exercise? Use the results to encourage you throughout this process and to clarify your planning.

Organization with the SMART Goal Framework

Now it's time to apply a framework to some of these goals. The SMART goal framework is commonly used throughout businesses and startups. It is updated here to be more relevant for performers, creatives, artists, and entertainers – with M, R, and T.

■ S is your goal specific (and satisfying)
■ M is your goal measurable (and money-making)
■ A is your goal action-based (and applicable to your vision)
■ R is your goal realistic (and what resources are needed)
■ T is your goal time-based (and how you will track it to observe progress)

Figure 1.4 shows an example. For a 6-month to 1-year goal, musician Chris wants to book more gigs.

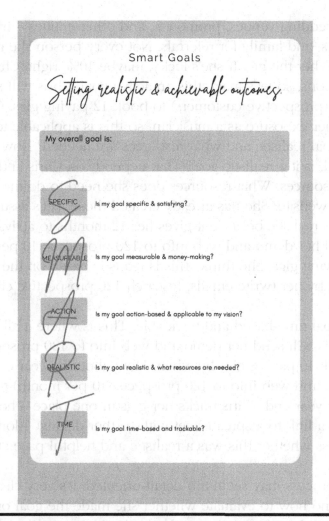

Figure 1.4 SMARTgoals by DeAngela Napier and Paula Landry.

S is your goal specific and satisfying. Instead of more, pick a number. Chris wants to book more gigs with her band to increase her pay. She knows that sometimes a free or almost free gig can lead to a paying job, but it can be time-consuming with no money, so she wants to focus more on paid gigs. This is an increase so it's satisfying.

M is your goal measurable and money-making. This goal is almost measurable – addressing that. Chris wants to book 12 gigs by year end and will be money-making if she stipulates PAYING gigs. Chris wants to book 12 paying gigs.

A is your goal action-based and applicable. Chris wants to book 12 paying gigs by year end. What actions can Chris take to book gigs? And what does she need to do the action? She could send information about herself out to clubs, wedding venues, promoters, and other entities – like colleagues, friends, and family for referrals. Not every person she reaches out to her will give her the gig. If she's lucky, maybe 10%, right. Chris can only control her actions, so let's make this an active goal. Chris will send info to 120 prospects (prospective customers) to book 12 paying gigs. Chris' vision is to level up her exposure as a musician, so this is applicable to her goals.

R is your goal realistic and what resources are needed? Now that there's action involved, is it a realistic goal? That depends on Chris and her time, energy, and resources. What resources does she need to do the outreach – a demo and a website? She has already created those. Let's assume this is January, so it is realistic because it gives her 12 months to activate this plan. Chris will send her demo and web info to 120 prospects (10 per month) to book 12 paying gigs. She thinks this is realistic based on the amount of effort required by her (write emails, research 120 prospective clients to send them to).

T is your goal time-based and track-able. This is where it all comes together – Chris will send her demo and web info to 120 prospects (10 per month) to book 10 paying gigs by when? How about by year end? Chris will send her demo and web info to 120 prospects (10 per month) to book 10 paying gigs by year end. Chris tracks her gigs in one place – her color-coded calendar (with a link to a spreadsheet with further details). Along the way she can reassess whether this was a realistic and helpful pace at which to work.

While the process may seem too detail-oriented, it's very clear what Chris needs to do, and how to evaluate whether she made the goal or not. With this level of planning, the results can be analyzed to see what did and didn't work, and then learn from that.

Take YOUR one or two primary goals and apply the SMART goal framework to each.

Often this will reveal that you need further steps, taking big goals, and making them into three smaller goals. Adding specific actions to each goal helps you get going. Taking your big goal and breaking it down into concrete actions can help if you are feeling overwhelmed. Do the next thing and that will keep you moving. If you're unsure of what actions to assign, it often means the goal is too big. Separate it into something more realistic until the actions become clear.

Whether you prefer physical notebooks, apps, or computer files to help manage your goals is your preference. Do what works for you. Apps like Trello offer a visual layout that may be helpful (Figure 1.5).

One Step At A Time

Use Tools That Work For You

Example of goal tracking in TRELLO software (trello.com)

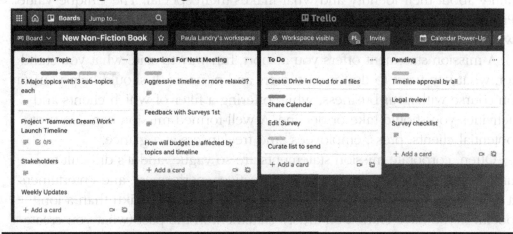

Figure 1.5   Goals In Trello by Paula Landry.

Ultimately, you will take one step at a time, action by action.

Articulating Your Vision

Humans are wired for storytelling. We tell ourselves the story of who we are, what we do, and why. We relate stories to ourselves, and others, of what is happening around us. We interpret the meaning of those events. Before we can articulate our creative business story to anyone else, we need to tell it to ourselves. There are several components, focus right now on your UVP – Unique Value Principle (why you're awesome), and the mission – what you're about, and the positive change you want to make.

Many professionals haven't clarified that vision to themselves, it's important. It's a solid step to set you in the right direction. This, along with your mission, will inform your startup and all the businesses that come from it.

If you don't like the story you tell yourself about yourself, take a few moments, and rewrite it. Make sure that it's empowering. Articulating your vision includes you as the first audience.

What are your superpowers? Write them down, this is what makes you unique – the UVP. In business, the UVP is only applied to what is sold, but it stems from the creator or generator, you! Creating a mission can be life-changing. Because once you identify why you're on this journey in the first place, it clarifies everything. When a company – or creative individual – has trouble gaining traction in the marketplace, it can go back to an uncertainty about their identity and what makes them special. The Unique Value Principle and Mission Statement are related, so it can be beneficial to play with them at the same time in order to amplify both.

A mission statement offers you a short, fun way to state what you stand for, what you want to do for customers and partners. It should help you stay on course with your business, while offering a filter of which clients and activities you should take or decline. A well-formed mission can convey to potential clients, press, employees, and freelancers at a glance.

Often, corporate mission statements are so vague, and it's difficult to understand what they do. For artists, creatives, performers, and entertainers, it is better to be short and sweet, more in the vein of a haiku than a long poem. If you have crafted an artist's statement in the past (what you create and why), your mission statement may share similar language and ideas. Take a few drafts and chop them down to the shortest most evocative statements.

Try to have fun with a mission statement, keep your personality in it. Have fun. Rather than merely listing what you want to do or sell, shift your focus to what guides and inspires you in your work.

Defining the UVP (Unique Value Principle)

Why you? Because you're awesome, hello! But what specifically makes you and your creative artistic abilities special? You may have a long list and you need to know it before you can communicate it to anyone else. Interesting, fascinating, enthralling? Pinpointing the ways you're unique will help you articulate why should someone trust you with their time, attention, energy, or money when you're selling services or products.

You can articulate your vision of what makes you special, also known as the UVP or Unique Value Principle. The UVP is why a customer is drawn to you. As you prepare what you're going to sell, you need to craft the UVP for that. It acts like a magnet between your products and services as opposed to anyone else. The UVP communicates your difference compared to some-one with a similar offering or skill set. It may take a while to pinpoint this and requires looking at your competition for comparison sake. Often this is a blend of your energy, your vibe, your aesthetic, values, beliefs, and world-view together.

For visual thinkers, you can discover your Unique Value Principle with a Word Cloud or mind map. These tools help you envision and connect thoughts, ideas, and feelings with language that, when put together, can crystallize into a concise phrase.

Exercise for creating a Word Cloud: Open a Word Cloud tool. There are many, such as:

https://www.wordclouds.com/
https://tagcrowd.com/
https://www.freewordcloudgenerator.com/

On a Word document, in a Word Cloud program, or on a blank page, notate the terms associated with you, your skills, talents, what excites you, and the following list. Then play with the design, fonts, and colors to create an excit-ing Word Cloud.

Write down a few words describing:

- Your creative abilities
- Your professional abilities
- Your related skills
- Your random talents
- What you love doing
- What you do well
- What people always ask you for help
- How you help people
- Emotions you wish to evoke with your creative work
- Product or service you could sell
- Sounds, smells, tools, colors, and materials associated with your work

Study the results. What sticks out once you've completed the Word Cloud? Pick out the words that truly resonate for you. They're telling you what makes you unique and helping to reveal your mission, even if you're not sure how they'll go together yet. There is something special in you, your way of seeing and being in the world that nobody else has (Figure 1.6).

Defning Your UVP

Unique Value Proposition

Figure 1.6   Word Cloud by Paula Landry.

After looking at it, write your UVP in your startup journal. You might come back to this if you want to.

Optional Exercise: Mind map. Often when you have a primary concept, you can generate many ideas related to it, branching out from that central idea to other directions. It's acceptable to utilize the words from what you've used in the previous exercise or start fresh.

Mind Map Template

- Get a large piece of paper (or use software) and draw a circle in the middle. Or create this online with an app like MindMup (https://app. mindmup.com/map/new).
- Decide what is your central intent or theme, like

- – My skills – professional, experience, training, innate, hobbies, interests
- – My creative business
- – Establish the first product or service
- – Find a new way to earn revenue
- – Build my brand
- ■ Write the theme in the center
- ■ Draw spokes around that primary circle, and attach a circle to each
  - – Label these circles with activities to help you achieve that primary goal, for instance, create a website, write an eBook, find a product to sell, attract work, generate fans, design a logo, create a visual brand, etc.
- ■ For each activity, again draw spokes from those circles and attach additional circles to the spokes, labeling them with ideas and activities to support them. The clusters are related ideas
  - – For example, around the word sales, you might have circles that say generate sales leads, qualify leads, write a newsletter, hire virtual assistants, build a website with eCommerce, sell in social media, offer webinars, networking, teaching, etc.
- ■ Keep drawing spokes and circles until you've run out of ideas for each activity
  - – Once complete, highlight the most important ones and start executing them. You'll get to them all in time

At this point, highlight the key concepts that stick out, what it is that makes you special, different, driven. Your Unique Value Principle should emerge by diluting the overall process into a short phrase.

What's Your Mission (Statement)?

After the following exercises, you have content to pour into your mission statement. It combines your UVP with values, beliefs, and guiding principles. The point of this is that your work has meaning, so that why you do this work – your mission – shines through. Edit it down to a phrase and something that is memorable, retaining only the most powerful emotional concepts. A mission statement is sometimes also referred to as a vision statement when you're working on a single creative project. This is a mini-story relaying what you're doing and why it matters to you. If you want to incorporate the impact you're hoping to achieve, great.

Short is better. It's more important that your mission statement act like a mantra – serving as a touchstone – both into your organization and outward to your market. So you can read it – "Why am I doing this? That's right, yes!" As well, this is something to share with the world so they understand what you're up to and why. In terms of length, succinct and vivid are better than long and flowery.

Here is an online tool to help you work on your mission statement if you need ideas: https://www.honeybook.com/mission-statement.

Here are some examples of mission statements:

■ We believe in making friends, not connections. We believe in sharing, not taking. We believe in celebrating others before celebrating ourselves
■ Stories have the power to change the world, so we want to amplify and shine a light on under-represented storytellers
■ We create strategies to help creative people share their originality and imagination with the world in a sustainable way

Mini Case Study. PANO (formerly NYC Women Filmmakers) is a non-profit organization that helps empower and educate women and non-binary film-makers. They were about to embark on a new direction planning a new, and ambitious, minimum viable product for their filmmakers and support-ers. The goal was to articulate not only what the organization stands for but also which tactics would be used. The organization worked with their board to contribute ideas and shape the meaning, the intent and feeling behind the statement. I volunteer on the board and was excited to see this unfold. Several people collectively created the statement, with each person weighing in. The result is a testament to the collaborative spirit in the group and clar-ity of vision. The resulting mission statement for NYC Women Filmmakers: We champion inclusion in film, TV, and media by connecting under-repre-sented creators with influential networks and valuable resources to impact meaningful change in the industry (NYCWomenFilmmakers.org).

This type of work is that of discovery, and you may be doing this solo. However, that doesn't mean you can't ask friends, colleagues, and peers for their opinions, feedback, and reflection. The process of understanding what makes you unique and your mission may take time. No worries! Create something with the understanding that they be updated at any time. For the purposes of galvanizing your startup, what is key for now is that you decide and move forward (Figure 1.7).

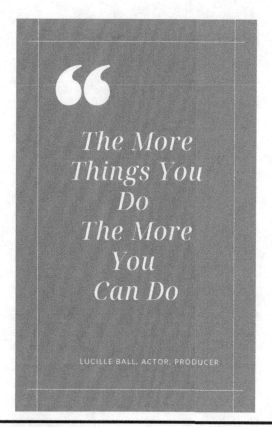

The More
Things You
Do
The More
You
Can Do

LUCILLE BALL, ACTOR, PRODUCER

Figure 1.7   Quote by Lucille Ball.

To wrap up your planning session, celebrate the work with an activity that is meaningful for you. Planning can provoke anxiety in some, as it signifies the intention to act. The mere fact you're reading these words means that you're up to the challenge. Now that you have created a direction and recognized the fire that fuels your work to some extent, the next step is to start building.

Chapter 2

Build and Test

Get ready to build something. Chances are good that it will be a bit messy and duct-taped together. That's fine. Wonderful, actually! You need to build a bunch of things to see what will work, and then get feedback. First from yourself and then from others. To get opinions on your startup ideas, you need to hear from the potential fans, audience members, potential clients, or customers who would buy or use your offering in the first place. Multiple times. The best feedback comes when your potential customer, client, fan, tribe member, follower, or audience can understand, see, try, or use what you're creating.

- What is building? Creating something to sell, quickly and cheaply
- What is testing? Trying your products or services to see what has promise
- Effective testing and building incorporate feedback when it makes sense

Feedback, before and during your building period, can help shape your concept into profitable offerings to sell. Responses from others get you out of your head. You don't want to build in a vacuum. Ask for opinions with surveys, or in conversations, texts, emails, or social media.

Building requires specificity – and by choosing certain things, you automatically discard others. You don't get the luxury of keeping your options open – you must be definite. Once you have a specific idea you can test it out by asking people what they think. Hearing their questions and comments will help you improve your concept. The point of this chapter is

DOI: 10.4324/9781003225140-2

to cultivate and curate concepts, with the ultimate goal of narrowing down and selecting one.

A head's up, this may get embarrassing. And that's okay. Craft an idea, and tell someone about it. When they respond, the feedback may be unexpected or painful. So put on your emotional armor for:

- Self-consciousness
- Stage fright
- Embarrassment at honest reactions
- Questions that shine a light on what you are still figuring out

Remember learning to walk? Probably you weren't that worried about how you looked because you wanted to get going. Self-doubt, imposter syndrome, and fear of embarrassing oneself have held many wonderful artistic makers from doing their thing. Don't let it hold you back.

Visualize and Recall Your Skills. You have innate talents that you bring to every task, even if they are not always top of mind. To move into this process with a success mindset, take a moment and recall something you've done when you were happily building something. Remember when you felt successful at managing time and money in any context and bring those feelings and positivity into this endeavor.

At any point during these tasks, if you get overwhelmed, feel self-doubt, or are struggling with time, take a moment. Breathe. Acknowledge your feelings, move your body. Shift the energy. Then get back to it. If this keeps happening, you may need to find some routine self-care so that you feel emotionally safe.

Caring for creatives. What can you do when you're feeling negative emotions that are standing in your way? Here are some ideas (Figure 2.1).

Find a ritual. Acknowledge your feelings. Write them down on a piece of paper. Maybe rip them up. Meditate, or chant to them. Visualize your ultimate goal. Remember why you are doing this in the first place and do it for yourself. Remember a time when you felt successful use that. Think about your role models. Find a visual touchstone to remind you of your creative superpowers! The world needs your beauty and distinct vision in the world. Reread your unique value proposition and mission statement.

Ask yourself if you are using emotions to procrastinate. Many artists use this as a tool, preferring to race toward an impending deadline. Some

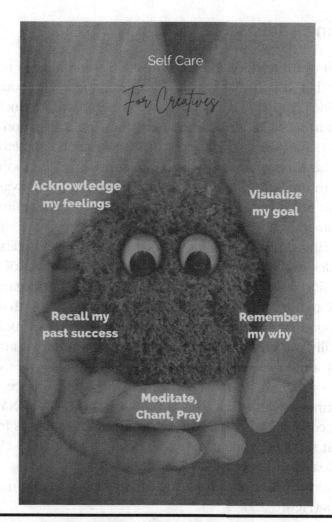

Figure 2.1   Self care. Google Eyes Photo by Ryan McGuire, CC0.

people use commitment devices, like promising to a friend they will complete a launch by a certain date. Mood and energy management are real, so give yourself permission to feel your feelings.

Tools: In order to keep your spirits up during this process, consider writing future texts and emails to yourself, scheduling them to arrive days and weeks ahead. These little notes and texts of encouragement may serve as a pleasant surprise and help remind you why this you are embarking on this journey.

Future Me is an online scheduled email service (www.futureme.org).

Text It Later is an online scheduled text service (www.textitlater.com).

Brainstorming – Ideas

Everything starts with an idea. Before you build something in real life, you must construct that in your imagination and on paper. With your list of artistic talents, abilities, and skills, it is time to come up with a bunch of ideas for your creative startup. Most ideas aren't new; they are a variation on a theme. With entertainers, performers, and creatives, this may be something more convenient for audiences, in a new place, or surprising due to the addition or subtraction of an unlikely element. A circus without animals was a bit new when Cirque du Soleil came onto the scene. Removing the animals, rather than adding something, made it unique. Of course, they have disrupted the traditional circus model in many ways, but that one is notable. Another example includes the Museum of Sex, which turned the idea of what a museum is, upside down. During the pandemic, many art organizations and artists got busy online, pivoting to digital experiences rather than in-person.

Idea conception is a no-judgment zone. Lock your editor/judge/critic/coach/inner bully out of the room and have a good time with the process.

Consider for a moment what brands, products, and services you're crazy about. What do you love to enjoy, consume, watch, experience, use, buy? Why? (I'm looking at you, Black Press Coffee on the UWS in NYC.) Then go the other way, consider what do you use and purchase that is frustrating. How could that service, product, or experience be improved? Use this lens toward your ideas and your buying habits.

Here are brainstorming techniques to generate potentially marketable and profitable ideas (Figure 2.2).

Tools

Your skills list. Paper or sticky notes, pen/pencil (write by hand – cursive if it's faster), timer (on phone, kitchen timer, whatever), music (optional). Refer to your primary and secondary skills list as discussed in Chapter 1, or create that now.

Exercises

1. Prep/setup (1–3 minutes)
   Turn on fun, upbeat music, or soundscape that makes you feel like a superhero. (Throwback songs from your glory days are highly encouraged.)
   (Can combine these)

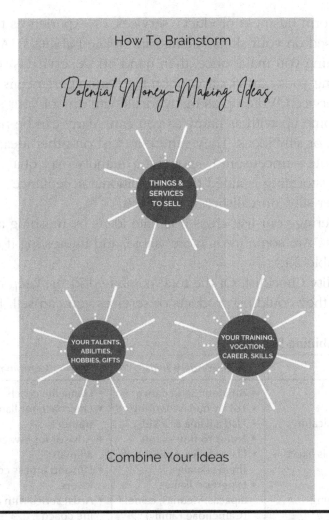

Figure 2.2   Brainstorming by DeAngela Napier and Paula Landry.

2. Take a vigorous deep breath, raise your eyes, grin
3. Stretch your hands up and into a V for victory high (power pose) over your head as if you're crossing the finish line in triumph. This boosts your confidence hormones

If you want to know about science, watch the Ted Talk by Amy Cuddy about body language.

I. DO: Your brain unleashed. Go as quickly as possible (no judgment)
   a. Set a timer for 5 minutes
      Glance at your skills list (or create one, if you can't find it from Chapter 1).

b. Brainstorm business products, services, or experiences that you can sell based on your skills, talents, and related abilities. (A product is something you make once, then hand off. A service is something requiring your participation upon use. An experience is a multi-layered service.) Write up as many ideas with any of your skills as you can. Come up with as many as you can. Many can be ridiculous, crappy, or silly ideas. They can be a twist on other ideas. The point is to write – uncensored – going for quantity over quality. This type of brainstorming is aided by unconditional acceptance of all ideas, however silly, unrealistic, or irrelevant.

c. Considering your list, cross-pollinate ideas by mushing a bunch together. Are some ideas more viable, and interesting if combined? (See Table 2.1.)

II. Marketability Checklist: Of the total combined ideas, keep those that seem like they could be products or services you can sell. Focus

Table 2.1   Combining Skill Sets

My primary skills	Secondary skills	Combinations
• Cartoonist • Visual artist • Good communicator • Good listener • My personality is like a life coach • Empathic, great listener – listening service? • Okay writer of dumb haikus • Can remember puns • Knowledge of art history from school • Proofread for friends • Good sense of design • Create resumes • Interested in a bit in chemistry for fun	• Amateur Salsa dancer • Lovely cursive writing • Had a llama as a kid • Non-pro fitness nut • Llama lover, nuts about them actually • Expert on llamas, alpacas, vicunas, camels (Camelidae Family) • Patient • Calm with animals and people • Fast cleaner in the house with lazy hacks • Created homemade non-toxic cheap cleaning solutions	• Llama life coach • Life coach for llama farmers/ trainers • Advisor for owners of large animals • Life and fitness coach for animal lovers • Artist series with a llama who's a life coach • Life coach for llama • Draw cartoon series – Fitness tips from a llama • Draw silly book – cleaning tips from a llama • Work with the author to make books about llamas • Write a series of llama haiku • Illustrate playing cards with llama • Teach kids how to draw • Make greeting cards with puns, haikus, and my art and sell • Graphic book about vicuna superhero • Sell my lazy, fast housekeeping secrets to students, moms

especially on those that would be relatively easy, fast, and cheap for you to create. Ask yourself which ideas are more marketable? Why would people want them? Pay attention to those concepts that seem easier to make and monetize than others.

III. Keep a list of the most promising in your startup journal to share for feedback. Compare results from your combined lists. Identify those that resonate the strongest with you within the frame of:
   - Money making
   - Fastest to generate
   - Which help people
   - What people want/need most
   - Cheap and easy to get going
   - Fun to do
   - I'm the person to offer this to the public

If you have several ideas but are lukewarm about them, pause. Think for a moment about what people always ask you to help them with. Think about your skills before going to sleep. See if your dreams will send you direction. Keep a notebook near your bed to capture any fleeting thoughts as you wake up.

Did you notice any themes? Do they address multiple skills of yours? Are your products or service ideas to sell quite specific, or very general? Be as specific as possible. If you're not sure your ideas are any good, don't worry. That's why we seek feedback. But if you're looking over your ideas and wonder how to build them, we can play with them a bit. Consider your favorites – could you multiply the product/service idea by 10? What would that look like? Or the opposite, could your idea be pared down to its essence? Examining the concept through a microscope, what is its most valuable feature?

Select your top three ideas for products or services to sell. The next step will be to define who would be most interested in paying you for them. Chances are good that you had a potential customer in your mind while you were working on this. Now it's time to bring them to the front.

What you are seeking is within you right now. There's no school you need to apply to, or special training necessary. You're seeking to blend your abilities to create an offering that people want to buy. It's akin to the Japanese term Ikigawa, a motivating force; something that gives a person a sense of purpose that comes from the sum of their skills, talents, and experiences, which is also profitable (Figure 2.3).

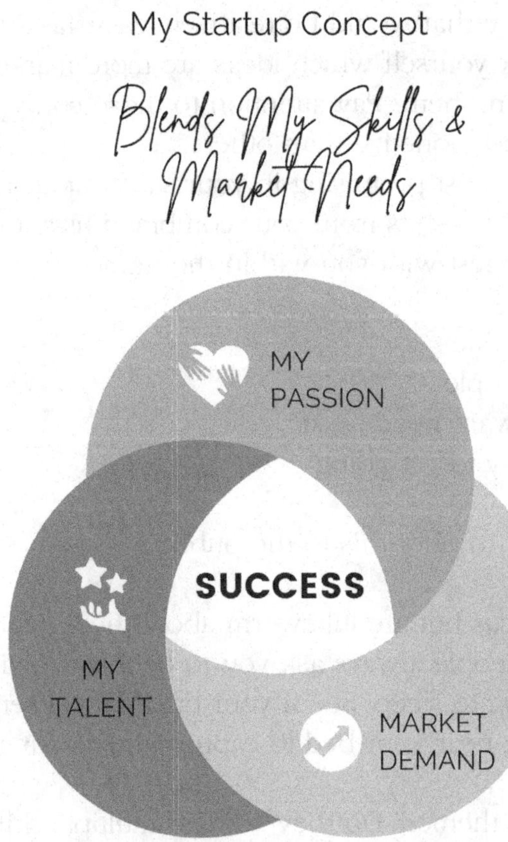
My Startup Concept
Blends My Skills & Market Needs
MY PASSION
SUCCESS
MY TALENT
MARKET DEMAND

Figure 2.3 Ikigawa by DeAngela Napier and Paula Landry.

There's nothing you have to change about yourself. Yes, you may need help and that's okay. Having said that, it will be a process of discovery. The first thing to do is find, build, and test just one thing to sell.

What makes a new concept profitable? It solves a problem or fulfills a need. It can be sold for a higher price than it would cost to buy or make. There is a clear customer base. In a perfect world, you can do much of that work independently for super cheap. Really profitable ideas tend to solve the most pain or fulfill the greatest need or desire (offering items that are rare, scarce or coveted). It's possible that what you sell doesn't solve a problem; but rather, adds value or inspires a feeling for your customer.

Building a Platform. If you are planning on building an online platform to attract advertisers, consider what you could sell to visitors first. In the platform model, such as a social media personality or an influencer, monetization happens once you build a big audience, then "sell" the eyeballs of that audience to brands or advertisers. In that way you have two customers.

Your customers who come to your platform to watch, listen, or engage with you (USERS) must come before the advertisers who will actually pay you. This is a business model of influencers and social media celebrities. If you must create a YouTube channel of 100,000 subscribers before you will earn any money, shift your thinking.

What could you actually sell to the visitors who come to your platform? Maybe the advertisers will or won't come eventually, but you don't want to have to wait for a long period of time to get going. The content you put up on your channel would be your actual Minimum Viable Product. One of the problems with the users/advertisers model (like with influencers) is that it may take a very long time to build a significant size of audience that you can monetize with advertisers. You want to think faster than that. What if you created videos (continuing the YouTube example) that lead up to someone buying something from you? In that way the channel serves as marketing as well as demonstration of your MVP.

Maybe you are a personal trainer. Your plan is to make fitness fun and family-oriented and you want to monetize that somehow. On YouTube, you create a channel with 10 exercises for families. You could then sell personalized exercise plans to families. Or sell personal training services for families. The point is not to discourage you from building a platform, but to think profits fast and first as you build your platform.

Never Been Done. If you believe your idea is so innovative that it's something "nobody has ever seen" before, or it's never been done, do lots of online searching. Use a variety of words in a different order. Very few ideas fall into this category. Most profitable ideas are an update or twist on something familiar. And there's no shame in that; in fact, it's AWESOME! Selling something truly novel requires the arduous work of educating customers, explaining what it is, why they need it, how to use it, and so forth. Better to shortcut all of that.

Defining Your Audiences

Who are your people/users/tribe/fans/clients/customers/buyers/followers? This is the essential question. Identifying whom you would like to deliver value to is at the heart of the entrepreneurial journey. This may not be obvious at first, and you may be part of this group.

Businesses refer to the terms *demographic* (external characteristics) and *psychographic* (internal characteristics) to describe buyers. However you describe them, get as specific as possible. It's important to ask exactly who needs and will buy my offering, before you spend time and energy building. These may be actual people you know or those with certain characteristics. If you have existing fans or an email list, this is a good place to start.

Grab your startup journal. Write down relevant details about your buyers. What do they need, want, and hope for? What is the value or fulfillment they are seeking? Remember that the "value" may not be something tangible, like a better mousetrap, or more compact umbrella; it may be a feeling. Many artists, performers, entertainers, and creatives don't have a customer in a straightforward manner, such as a brick-and-mortar store has a person coming in to buy a specific product sitting on a shelf. Define your customers with as much detail as possible. The terminology for your buyers will vary depending on your industry. The terminology is less important than your conception and understanding of them.

Jot down the most relevant traits about your potential customer. Demographics – external factors, or psychographics – internal factors (the most important, typically), geography, or buying behaviors. Don't get hung up on whether you know every single aspect of that person or not (Figure 2.4).

Different Types. For some businesses, there are two different groups of customers, one group buys directly from you, individuals, or companies. Tailor your MVP to buyers. This is often thought of as business-to-consumer (B2C), it's a direct relationship. Some artists have indirect relationships with customers, like the platform model referenced earlier. In this model, you build a following, attracting fans, clicks, and subscribers. It's the advertisers who will actually pay you money (a B2B relationship – business-to-business) through platforms like YouTube. It's necessary to build a following before you can secure advertisers. That model is valid, but time-consuming. If you must attract 100,000+ people to your site or page until you can generate revenue, who knows how long that will take. In the meantime, consider the following you are trying to attract in the first place – Can you actually sell something to the people in this group? What value can you bring to them that THEY might compensate you for and therein become customers? It's worth considering and may generate revenue on the way to reaching the 100,000 and also cashing in on advertising.

Everyone is my customer. If you say "everyone will want my _____, once it's created," well …. maybe. But probably not. "Everyone" in the world is very tough to market to. You really want to sell to the exact people who

Describe My Customers

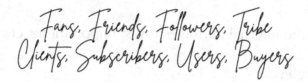

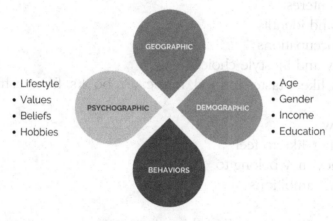

Figure 2.4   Who Are My Customers by DeAngela Napier and Paula Landry.

want what you are selling. Niche audiences with defined characteristics are your best bet.

Grab your startup journal and write all the relevant details about your buyer that you know presently.

Demographic information (certain categories are helpful):

- Where do they live (geography, which may be general or specific)
- Gender
- Age
- Education level
- Income level

- Single/married
- Raising kids or not

Psychographics, the internal attributes (most important for entrepreneurs):

- Where in life cycle
- Priorities and dreams
- Beliefs, hobbies, and interests
- Political leanings and religion
- Causes of interest
- Activities and identity
- Types of occupations
- Personality and lifestyle choices
- What they like – tastes in food, music, art, books, film, fashion, shopping
- World view
- How do they like to feel
- Groups they may belong to
- Aspirational ambitions

Whether you know most or all of this information doesn't matter. The point is to have a strong feel for your buyers.

Problem/Solution Approach versus What They Want. The prevailing thinking in the startup space is based around "solving a problem" for someone. That can work for certain business ideas. However, in the artistic and creative realms, this may not apply.

If you don't perceive a "problem" for your audience, substitute the problem with needs or desires. These could be physical, emotional, or spiritual. They may even be convenience and time related, or aspirational and inspirational. Buyers purchase a painting, song, jewelry, or movie for purely aesthetic and enjoyment, curiosity, buzz, or any other reason.

I will help solve this problem (or need, desire or want) _____
_____ for these people (describe briefly)_____
_____. I will bring them value with my _____
_____.

It may help to examine your purchasing habits. Ask yourself, what are the reasons I select artistic or fashion items to purchase? Music or decorations, food, and personal services? A buyer is seeking a feeling, vibe, a look. A feeling of belonging or wanting to feel younger, free, wild, sexy, new and different, adventurous, rich and important, smart, and together. If you look at movies, music, art, clothing, makeup, beauty treatments, gym memberships, and so many things, we're purchasing an idea of ourselves. Tap into that.

Surveys are a way to ask opinions from others. They are easy to use, shareable via email, text, messaging, and on social media. The more the feedback, the better.

Survey Tools

Get used to reaching out to potential customers during this journey. Great ideas don't thrive in a vacuum, they need the living energy from input. The purpose of sending a survey at this juncture is to receive feedback about your ideas. Surveys aren't the only way, but they are affordable and efficient.

Alternatives. Ask anyone about your idea. Talk to other humans. Ask pointed questions – What do you think of this business idea? Would you pay for it? It may feel awkward at first, but you become used to it. There's nothing like a face-to-face or phone conversation, for in-depth idea exchange. That's because the conversation is somewhat collaborative in nature to begin with.

In-the-moment feedback delivers on sensory levels – tone of voice, eye contact, thoughtful response, or quick instinctual answer. Anytime you must explain your idea it will help you understand it better yourself.

Gird your loins. Please put on your emotional suit of armor during this process. You may hear things that you don't want to – things that are critical or discouraging. Don't let that deter you! The world needs your creations.

Market research can be primary or secondary. Primary comes straight from the source, this is gold. Secondary means you're getting the information second-hand (like searching online).

Surveys are great because you can send them at your convenience, and the participant may fill them out at their convenience. They are low cost, low touch, and low time commitment. Technology allows us to see graphical interpretation of the information, parse by customer attributes, and offer respondents a way to stay anonymous.

1. Create the survey; send it to potential fans, customers, and clients; then implement the relevant findings if they make sense. Keep most questions short and direct, like the example shown in Figure 2.5.

Services. The best tools include free and easy services such as Survey Monkey, Typeform, Google Forms, and Mailchimp. Use whatever tools you

Survey Question Example

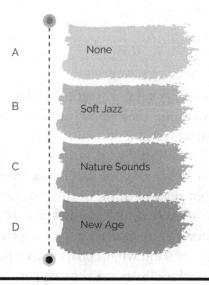

#1 What kind of music do
you enjoy during
yoga class?

A   None

B   Soft Jazz

C   Nature Sounds

D   New Age

Figure 2.5   Survey Questions by Paula Landry.

like best. Go for free and if you need more buzzers and whistles, then add a
paid service later on.

Plan on sending four to five surveys over your initial entrepreneurial process. These are good junctures to request feedback:

1. Build and test. For confirmation of idea selection and MVP concept
2. Create with constraints. For feature refinement into product/service
3. Share with awareness. To shape marketing concept and price point
4. Launch and generate. For reactions to MVP (Minimum Viable Product),
   improvement, and future offerings
5. Manage and analyze. To get additional opinions on next steps
6. Yearly survey

Survey Basics. Surveys consist of a short list of questions. Send to several
people because you won't get responses from everyone: 10% is a decent
response, and 4–5% is the norm.

Here are steps for designing your survey:

1. Start the survey with a concise and brief paragraph of context that explains why you're asking for their time and attention
2. Create time parameters for urgency or a due date
3. Write 5–10 questions pertaining to your concept. Keep it brief with varied formats and easy answers (True/false, Multiple choice, check-boxes)
4. Define the goal, what do you need to know right now? Build questions that reveal this information (could be about a concept, buying habits, and pricing)
5. Open an account on Survey Monkey (or other free platforms)
6. Include an open-ended question for unstructured ideas from your participant so that the respondent can write freely about their opinions
7. Capture a bit of demographic/psychographic data in one to two questions
8. Check for bias by asking questions that don't forecast the answers you want. One way to avoid this is to ask a friend to look it over you don't telegraph exactly what you want a recipient to answer
9. Test by sending it to yourself a few times at a different email address to see what it looks/feels like to you. Include thanks at the end
10. Send to as many potential customers as possible (via email, social media, and text)
11. Analyze the results. Did you learn something? Implement that into your business concept. If you need more information and feedback right away because the results were ambiguous, revise, and then send to another group (not the same group, you don't want to be spammy)
12. Get in the habit of sending surveys out with some regularity, but not more than one time every other month or so. People will stop responding if they feel spammed (Figure 2.6)

Initially, a reason to do a survey is to help you understand if people are interested in buying your concept. Collect and organize your feedback in your startup journal.

Example of Feedback Document. Figure 2.7 shows a very basic example of one way to organize a feedback document:

Here's what feedback should do:

■ Focus on your ideas
■ Offer motivation and momentum
■ Help you pinpoint the right people as customers
■ Give you insight as to the right product or service

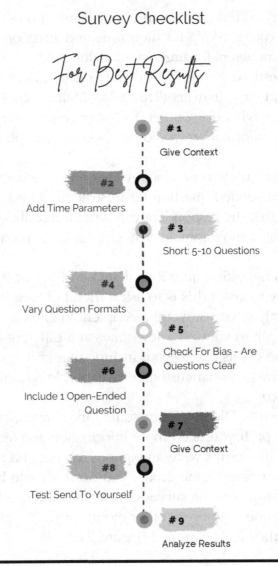

Figure 2.6   **Survey Checklist by DeAngela Napier and Paula Landry.**

Here's what feedback shouldn't do:

- Make you feel bad (this is all information to learn from; it's not personal)
- Put negative pressure on you
- Compare you unfavorably to others

Something you may learn from survey results is that you didn't ask the right questions and people were confused, or your communication was unclear.

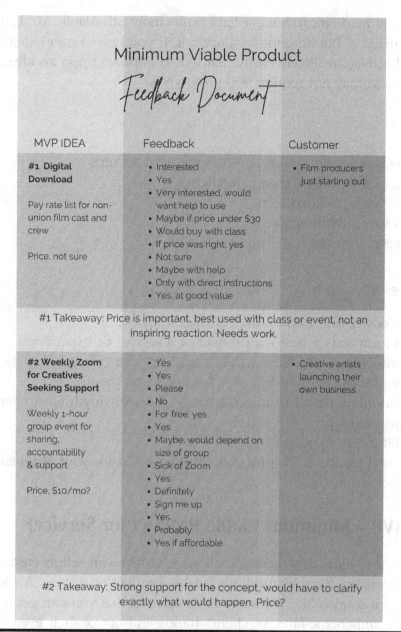

Minimum Viable Product
Feedback Document

MVP IDEA	Feedback	Customer
#1 Digital Download Pay rate list for non-union film cast and crew Price, not sure	• Interested • Yes • Very interested, would want help to use • Maybe if price under $30 • Would buy with class • If price was right, yes • Not sure • Maybe with help • Only with direct instructions • Yes, at good value	• Film producers just starting out
#1 Takeaway: Price is important, best used with class or event, not an inspiring reaction. Needs work.		
#2 Weekly Zoom for Creatives Seeking Support Weekly 1-hour group event for sharing, accountability & support Price, $10/mo?	• Yes • Yes • Please • No • For free, yes • Yes • Maybe, would depend on size of group • Sick of Zoom • Yes • Definitely • Sign me up • Yes • Probably • Yes if affordable	• Creative artists launching their own business
#2 Takeaway: Strong support for the concept, would have to clarify exactly what would happen. Price?		

Figure 2.7   Feedback Document by Paula Landry.

This doesn't reflect necessarily on your concept. Also, if several recipients make similar comments several times, look into it further.

You may have read that Thomas Edison created 900 prototype light bulbs before he got it right. Awesome. But another famous inventor, Lewis Latimer, an African-American self-educated inventor, improved on the design, by producing a carbon filament that was more durable and longer lasting. This improvement made incandescent light bulbs more affordable. Mr. Latimer didn't re-invent it, but he improved upon it. If you have a good idea that you could activate relatively easily that would improve upon an idea, that's awesome, and may not require 900 prototypes.

Tools

- https://simpletexting.com/sms-text-message-surveys/
- https://www.podium.com/campaigns/
- https://www.slicktext.com/
- www.surveymonkey.com
- simpletexting.com

Exercises

- Write down your two to three strongest ideas
- What form suits it best – a product or a service or experience
- Describe the person who would want/use your offering. Are there many of these people? Where would you find them?
- Search online for a few minutes to see if there's anything similar
- Create a survey
- Send it to 10–30 people
- With that feedback, choose your strongest idea for your Minimal Viable Product

Your MVP – Minimum Viable Product (or Service)

Once you have ideas and feedback about what you can sell to customers, refine the concept for your minimum viable product or service. An MVP is just what it sounds like, the most basic offering that you can get into a customer's, audience's, fan's, or client's hands, in front of their eyes, ears, or whatever – for them to try it. The viability part is that it works, even on a basic level. The value in this is that it's not theoretical at this point. You'll receive real feedback. "This is great!" Or "I don't understand, it's not working, why does it…." Your MVP will help you learn.

A proponent and thought leader in the lean startup concept (and author of the fantastic book *The Lean Startup*), Eric Ries sites that a great minimal viable product will allow you to "collect the maximum amount of validated learning about customers with the least effort."

Examples include a basic membership website with three to five essential features. Your plan may be to include many more features, but the first iteration (version) gives a taste of everything to come. It has essential functions. Other examples include a table of contents and first chapter for your eBook, a video trailer or a few sessions of a new online class, and a basic website with concept art. For visual artists, an MVP may be a portfolio or Instagram page filled with your work. A video web series MVP may consist of a pitch deck with graphics, a synopsis, and character sketches. For movies, it may consist of a poster with vivid artwork and a description of the plot of your movie. If you're building an app, you may make a free version on Glide with three to five essential features. Performers may record a scene or an evocative moment from a script.

You need enough for a customer to try out, it doesn't have to be loaded with features, but it must have enough features to be viable. It's important to seek some balance between minimum and viable. The point of the "minimum" is to get it out the door fast and affordably, then get it in your fans' hands for feedback. Your vision may include ultimately 100 features (pages, artworks, creations, clothing designs, photos, etc.) if it's too minimum and it's not enough (that's the viable part) you'll miss out on gaining more customers and getting traction. Balance is key, but action is best.

Mini Case Study. Bryan Steele. Professional Saxophonist, professional musician, and composer Bryan Steele could see at the outset of his musical career in New York City that performing on sax was great, but narrow. He wanted to make sure that his future included more opportunity, financial promise, flexibility, and longevity. Electronic music and composing on a personal computer at the time was new, and somewhat daunting, but he recognized it as the future and a way into broadened possibilities. Amid gigging, teaching, networking, and performing, Bryan composed songs, recording them on his equipment, essentially teaching himself how to use the technology. His MVP – minimal viable offering – consisted of those first individual songs, which were written, recorded, mixed, and shared with the world. He jumped in, focusing on one thing at a time. Each song improved. It was clear there were many things involved, but he focused on one action, learning each skill as needed. He became more skilled in playing, composing, and orchestration subsequently learning the appropriate software for recording and mixing music, then became versed in distributing, and marketing his songs. Each recording increased in quality. He learned more about the technology.

The learning was in service of his goals – selling songs, building a musical career as a professional musician. No matter what was going on, even while on tour for the award-winning Broadway musical *Moving Out*, Bryan wrote music. He shows up every day and works, whether it's playing, recording, writing, or administrative duties. His work ethic is an important aspect of his success. As he progressed, he built his catalog of music, pursuing opportunities in the television, film, and commercial world. He learned to listen to his customers – and what they needed and were seeking in film scores, TV programs, and jingles (Figure 2.8).

Enjoy his music and connect with him at https://bryansteele.net/music, on Spotify, Apple Music, and more.

Exercise: What behavior could you learn from Bryan Steele and adapt for yourself? If you were modeling his example, how could you apply it to creating your MVP?

Products and Services

Look in your startup journal at your best ideas. Choose the one that got the best feedback from audiences and seems potentially profitable. Describe it in

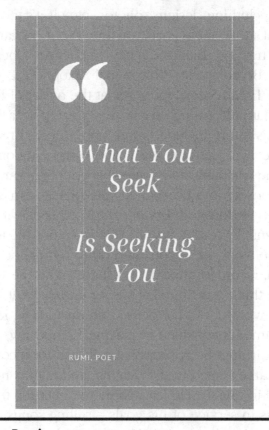

Figure 2.8 Quote by Rumi.

as much detail as possible, how it looks and works. What form should your idea take – a product, service, or experience; something physical or digital? Once you do it the first time, the process will get easier. If your creation is an experience – where you interact live with an audience, then it most likely is a service. Experiences are almost always a form of service, because you are involved in it in real time (whether in person or live-streaming). Products, services, and experiences may take different forms (Figure 2.9).

An example of services: if you perform clowning, you could stage an actual performance (live or online) or teach clowning arts. Products include selling your own juggling balls. An experience might consist of something like a clowning party where the participants pay for and use your juggling balls and are entertained as they learn how to juggle in real time.

If it's a product, what is the tangible form? Would it be a one-time thing to buy or something that's a repeated purchase, like a subscription? How

Product vs. Service vs. Experience

What Is The Difference

PRODUCT	SERVICE	EXPERIENCE
• Form	• Benefit	• Live Event or
• Specific Use /	• My Involvement	Online
Customer	• Customer	• Event Interaction
Interaction	Interaction	• In Real Time
• My Limited	• "Where" It	• Audience Size
Involvement	Happens	• Multi-layered
• Shipping /		Service
Logistics		

Figure 2.9 Product, Service, Experience by DeAngela Napier and Paula Landry.

does it feel or look? How is it used? Is there packaging? Does it expire or wear out and have to be replaced? Are there a few parts to it – with a consumable? (Like a printer – you buy that one time, but you need to keep buying ink – the ink cartridge is the consumable.) Imagine your product as clearly as possible.

If your offering is a service, how does it benefit people? Where do they get it and how would they use it? What is the minimum service they could use? What is my involvement in that interaction? How long does it last?

If your offering is an experience, what does it consist of? What are the various real-time components? Are there related products? Can the experience be tilted into different types of participants? Is there any part of the experience that would not be real time? When would that take place? Where does it live?

Describe these to yourself relating to your ideas and find the product or service that stands out. Commit to creating it, identify the help you might need, and come up with a (short) timeline that will spur you forward with urgency. For those struggling with what to create, reflect on what you enjoy making. Ask yourself questions around that:

■ What kinds of products do I like, enjoy, consume, and benefit from?
■ Why?
■ How do they improve my life?
■ What kind of customers will I be selling the product to?
■ What value would it provide for them?
■ Do you personally know customers who'd be interested in buying this?
■ Is the market large enough to be profitable?

Figuring out this takes thought, and looking around the marketplace to see what is out there already. REMEMBER you don't have to create something so original that nobody has ever seen it before.

In your startup journal, describe your MVP product, service, or experience. Once you have clarity on that, you will want to imagine various features of it, how they benefit users. Benefits are what a consumer is typically interested in. They want to understand how they specifically benefit. Various features contribute to these benefits, as explained in Table 2.2.

Think of products as anything you create and don't have to be involved with for the person to use once the person buys something. Tangible goods are products and may be digital or physical. An example would be if you wrote and designed a coloring book. A physical version would be the

Table 2.2 Features and Benefits

Feature of what you're selling	Benefit to the buyer
A feature is what something is	A benefit is what something does
A distinction or noticeable quality	Anything that is helpful or advantageous
Something offered as a special attraction	Something that contributes to or increases well-being for a buyer
Secondary reason for buying	Primary reason for buying
Ways that it's unique from competitors	Feeling, convenience, lifestyle, identity

tangible coloring book that someone could buy in a book store, a digital version would be the PDF file of a printable coloring book that the person prints and uses at their convenience. Product examples include books, graphic wallpaper designs, pre-made graphics, apps, video games, the recorded performance of a song, original artworks, and prints of artwork.

Typically we think of products as actual real-world physical objects that can be touched, smelled, felt, and even seen. However, products can have both a physical and, or, a digital form. If you are a photographer, you may capture an image on a camera. You may print that image out, frame it, and sell it to someone at an art fair. That is physical. A digital version would be if you then sell or license the file of that image in a digital format online at Shutterstock, or other online photo marketplaces for someone to use however they like.

Services require your ongoing involvement or participation. Whether that is a live performance, generally that consists of you DOING something for someone. That someone may be a person, group of people, or company. You may be doing that service in real time for them – whether that is teaching live juggling lessons to them, designing a shirt, baking them a cake, creating a personalized digital print, etc. The service may be something you complete, alone, but it is generated for a specific entity within a specified period of time. A service requires you, generally in real time (although not always). For example, if you teach an online course, that is a service you provide. Your meetings may be synchronous (in real-time students and teacher meets) or asynchronous (students do assignments, then get feedback by the teacher at regular intervals). Experiences are usually multi-layered services. Examples of services include a guided walking tour with snacking at various establishments during the tour, live party performances incorporating interactive cooperation; drawing or painting a portrait while wine-tasting, and live workshops incorporating companion products.

It is possible for your offering to be both. A digital artist on Instagram transforms and personalizes clients' photographs transforming them into comic-book stylized digital images. This is both a product and a service. The service she offers in the personalization of YOUR actual photos, and the product would be the resulting images the artists send to the client once they are transformed. The most important thing is that you know exactly what you are creating. Understand where you will sell it, how your customers will access it after they have made the purchase.

As a rule of thumb, a product does not need your ongoing, direct interaction with a customer, while a service (and experience) usually does.

Passive Income, Recurring Income, Design Once, Sell Multiple Times

The concept of passive income is something that generates income for you while you sleep. It's a great idea but in reality, lots of things must happen before you go to bed – i.e. – passive part.

However, what this really refers to are products that you create one time, and they can be sold, ongoing, to several customers, without your direct presence. You don't have to ring up the sale, ship it, handle logistics, and directly manage delivery to your customer and their use of the item. There's nothing passive about promoting and marketing your products, answering customer questions or prospective customer questions, dealing with returns if that happens, and securing reviews and referrals.

One goal for an offering is something that generates recurring income. Typically this is done on a subscription basis. If you could create something once and get paid multiple times, that would create time efficiencies. Recurring income may sustain your startup through lean times. In a sense, a subscription could function like passive income and recurring revenue. Not everything works in a subscription model, so if it's not a fit, don't force it.

One of the appeals with digital products, and subscription items, is that you create it one time, but sell it several times. (Spoiler alert, you'll probably keep improving it.) If you can front-load the work in exchange for multiple sales and recurring revenue, that is an advantage.

An example of recurring revenue is a recorded song. You could upload your digital file version of the song to sell on your website. You could upload the song to a platform like BandCamp where others could buy it. You could submit the song to Pandora or CDBaby where customers could stream it, and you'd earn a royalty for those streams. If you uploaded the song to YouTube, it could get played many times and you might earn money from ads played adjacent to the song. After a while this product – your song – that you created one time – will create passive income after you've uploaded it to several platforms. You don't have to push it into the hands of listeners (although you will continue to promote). You could sell a physical version of the song on a CD, vinyl album, or cassette tape, or even as a file on a thumb drive.

A subscription relating to this product could be an intensive "making of" service, where you videotape yourself writing the song, how you did it, what the process was, structure, selecting the tracks, musicians, orchestrating the song, recording it, as you point out how a viewer may do that themselves. By breaking this intimate video lesson into 20 segments – a subscription model may be aspiring musicians subscribing on a monthly basis to receive a weekly video lesson with exercises or instructions to do it themselves. The limits are based on your imagination.

Physical

Physical offerings are products. When a fashion designer creates a dress specifically for one client, it will yield both a product (the dress) and the service of designing it to the customer's specifications. The same could be said for commissioned works of craftspeople (woodworkers, jewelry designers, fine artists). A disadvantage of selling a physical product is when you have to spend money purchasing, handling, and storing inventory. Physical products usually require money spent prior to generating income, so you will need to constantly estimate future sales to help you decide how much inventory to order.

There are a number of Print-on-Demand (POD) online services. This allows your customer to select a product as you designed it, but it's only manufactured at the moment someone makes the purchase. This eliminates the expensive issue of buying, creating, and storing inventory. Platforms that offer POD include:

- Shopify
- RedBubble
- Printful
- Society6
- SPOD
- Printify

- Apliiq Dropship
- Teelaunch
- CustomCat
- Lulu Xpress
- Threadless

If you are actually inventing a physical product, you may need a patent to protect your concept. Chapter 5 covers why and when someone would need a patent, and what the overall process is.

When you are selling digital products, you don't have an inventory issue, however, there are other considerations.

Digital

The availability of fast and reliable Internet access, along with the proliferation of tablets, personal computers, and mobile phones means that most people are active consumers in the digital economy. Audiences and buyers of all walks of life now are comfortable buying digital versions of things. You as a creator have the option to create and sell a digital MVP. Digital delivery avoids inventory altogether. However, it's important to ensure that the logistics and technical delivery of your digital product is working.

Examples of digital products include any computer file that can be downloaded from a mobile or computer app to any type of digital file. File formats may include images, movies, text-based files, or something else. Where you present or sell your work is a trade-off; free platforms give less control, paid offer more control. In the streaming realm, where music and video are prominent, your business may rely on third party software that you don't control (Vimeo, BandCamp, CD Baby, etc.). Decisions around this are finding the right platform, and setting it up so it works best for you. Digital offerings could include:

- Consulting service with clients on specific topics
- Providing advice, counseling, and insights
- Offering in-real-time creation of artwork online
- Styling service and fitness coaching
- Conducting training, teaching, and live performances
- Working with a group to learn, for games or social interactions

Some creatives license their intellectual property (writing, images, music, moving images) to others. There are stock media sites (Shutterstock, Getty,

Pond5) solely for this use. Rather than selling the work outright, they sign a licensing agreement which controls and limits certain rights. A trend in the digital marketplace includes experiences and products like NFTs, based on the blockchain technology.

NFT/Blockchain. With the explosion of the digital sphere, the concept of "originals" was lost. If digital replicas are identical, then what does it matter if something was the "first"? That concept has been reclaimed with NFTs, which embrace the spirit of digital originals and digital collections. NFT stands for non-fungible token, which means that it's unique and can't be replaced with something else. NFT is based on blockchain technology. What is exciting about NFTs is the idea that digital creators – who typically create exact copies of something – can generate increased value by auctioning and selling unique digital creations. Here are some of the terminologies:

- NFT – Non-fungible token (a unique digital asset)
- Decentralized – No middle person, such as any blockchain-based system that is designed to remove intermediaries between transacting parties. The idea is transactions with transparency, accountability, and security
- Blockchain – A digital system of technology record-keeping. NFTs utilize the underlying blockchain system. Blockchain was designed to increase the security, transparency, and efficiency of transactions utilizing a decentralized system in order to transfer digital items of value
- Bitcoin is a digital currency based on the blockchain system. It was made to be an alternative to national currencies as a medium of exchange and a store of value
- Ethereum – It uses blockchain technology with varied functionality and is the basis for many NFTs and other blockchain media-related ventures

A bitcoin is fungible – trade one for another, and you'll have exactly the same thing. A one-of-a-kind item of jewelry, or trading card, is non-fungible. NFTs can be anything digital, but the current excitement is around using the tech to sell digital artworks and experiences.

What does this mean for creatives? If it is a fit, you may be able to create and sell your work as an NFT on an NFT Marketplace. While not recommended as the first place to sell your MVP, this space is developing quickly and may be a fit for what you do. NFT Marketplaces include:

- SuperRare.co
- MakersPlace

- Rarible
- OpenSea
- Nifty Gateway
- ASYNC
- hiç et nuna
- Known Origin

Experiences

Many entertainers, performers, and artists sell experiences, an extension of services. They could have personalized, including intimate concerts, interactive workshops, performing or creating in front of an audience. The more interesting an experience can be, the better it is. The point is to draw your audience into what you're doing as much as possible, whether in real life or on the Internet. A key element of experiences is involving the audience in the process, so they feel part of whatever it is that you're creating. There are an infinite amount of possibilities, such as on Instagram live and other social media live-streaming services. To clarify, this is not about your "professional experience" as a career, but this is defining a specific tailored activity to sell that a customer could participate in. As an example, a fresh lasagna sold in a restaurant is a product, delivering it to your home is a service, but the chef actually arriving on the doorstep, making that lasagna fresh from the oven to customers in their home, with candles, music, and describing all the ingredients and how it was made, would be an experience.

Designing and Creating Your Offering

An offering is a succinct articulation of what you want to sell, to whom, and how it benefits your fans, audiences, or clients. Writing this and saying it a few times can help you hone in on your idea. You want to be able to express it quickly and vividly. When you feel that it's right, add what makes your offering unique. This is more powerful than just stating what you sell. Come up with the best way to express it, then get feedback from a few people to see if they understand it.

Define what you're offering: I can sell _____ to these people _____ (briefly describe them) which

will help them _____ (specific benefits
of buying) and makes them feel _____. This offering is
unique _____ (how it's unique/special).

Let's find an example – so you may have the skills of an interior designer who
can transform any space into something lovely. Great skill, very specific. You
have an eye for beauty, space, and aesthetic sense – Can you put that into
something aside from interior decorating? If you wanted to sell a digital product right away, could you distill your process into a repeatable set of steps?
Could you create and sell color palettes of the moment? Begin a consulting
service for young professionals to help them with easy, fast style tips? Anyone
with this kind of skill set probably has many related skills pertaining to style in
their home, but also around organizing and de-cluttering, creating systems of
efficiency. This person probably could also put colors together someplace else
like as related to wardrobe, or knows how to stretch a designing budget, possibly staging a home for sale, assisting with a make-over for a tiny apartment?
Many decorators have great Photoshop skills, can shop quickly and decisively
(don't under-rate this, it's definitely a skill), and can source high-end pieces in
thrift stores. So your inter-related skills (people-person, pet-oriented, specializes in holiday décor) could lead you to something people want to pay for.

As an example, if you are a graphic or visual artist, would it be possible
to sell copies of originals to many people, or could you license your work to
companies for their marketing. Think of ways that your creative skills may
be useful in a different context or business setting. You are adapting your
skills and vision to various audiences whom you may not have considered
previously. When it's difficult to identify which skills you can draw from, ask
yourself specific questions:

- Do I have more than one type of artwork to sell
- What is unique about my work compared to others
- Which audiences tend to be drawn to my artwork
- Why are they interested
- Are there others who share that same interest – for a different reason or
  context
- Can I modify my work to better appeal to those other markets without
  changing the character inherent in my work

Getting into the head of your potential customers, what they hate, love, and
want can help you find the right MVP. People buy things to improve upon a

feeling – to look, feel, sound, appear better in some way. Why do we buy? Often it's not need-based, it's a wish, hope, want, desire – and what does that fulfill? Seeking a certain feeling.

Before you do a ton of work to build something, keep talking to people as you build out the concept to get in the customer's mind.

The best business opportunities come from people's direct wants and needs. People have physical, emotional, and spiritual needs and you're tapping into one or all of them. With many types of art, entertainment, performances, and media tap into interests, you're not only eliminating boredom and creating diversions but also filling an emotional need. A thirst to feel a certain way.

> People want and need what I am offering because it helps them
> _____ (emotional needs, physical needs, convenience, eliminate other problem).
> People will benefit from what I am offering in this way
> _____, and _____
> (emotional needs, physical needs, convenience, other).
> Two notable features of my offering include _____ and
> _____.
>
> Remember the UVP – your unique value or your work, skills, and talents? Now apply that to your offering. Define what is unique about what you are selling. My offering is unique because _____
> _____ (unique value proposition).

No matter what type of performer or creator you are, stretch your ideas of what you can make or do. If you create something you can sell the original, copy the original and sell those, teach others to make it in a book or video or online class, teach a live workshop or class to make it, share your experience of why and how you created that and how it changed you. You can teach people in a group experience to create and enjoy the group process. You can hold live/online events to speak or share your experiences empowering others to do the same. You can offer a personal connection with people (like consulting) to aid them in their goals around this. You can partner with a sponsor or brand that would like to be showcased, or affiliated with, your work.

Think of what you do with an entirely different audience, online and in real life, in a completely different setting.

As you're creating your prototypes working toward your MVP, make notes so you remember what works and what doesn't (this can blur together so detailed notes are important). The main themes to keep in mind while building several prototypes on the way to your MVP are:

1. Keep your mindset audience/customer-focused, think about who you're creating for
2. Get data-driven, quantify whatever you can in the process so you can learn from it
3. Marketability test. If nobody wants it, there's no point in putting lots of time and energy into selling it
4. Good, quickly is better than perfect to get whatever you are building into the user's hands
5. When you think about who might use what you're creating, ask if the group is easily defined. And is it big enough? There's no point in creating something for only two customers on the planet
6. Make sure your solution is better than and different from what's already out there. It doesn't have to be wildly different – just different enough
7. Ask for opinions about the idea from people you know who are in the audience or population for your business
8. Once you have your MVP ready, you'll ask them to test it for you free, in return for confidentiality and feedback

Legal Considerations at the Start. Will someone steal my idea? Probably not. In the first place, an idea alone isn't something you can copyright, but the execution or expression of an idea is. As your offer is a work in progress, it's important to maintain momentum in building your startup. However, legally protecting your intellectual property at some point is important. Chapter 6 covers this in more detail. When in doubt, contact an attorney who specializes in intellectual property and entertainment.

Now that you've defined your offer, and started building, it's time to create it. To do so, you'll have to consider what resources are needed, how to manage the overall process.

Building Steps. Your first stage is laying out the schedule to finish your MVP. The idea is to get moving rapidly to get something out the door quickly. But there's no doing that until you have a plan.

Game plan. My MVP will be due by _____. The actions I'll take to complete it include the following:

Step 1 : Action   Due date   How I'll Celebrate
Step 2 : Action   Due date   How I'll Celebrate
Step 3 : Action   Due date   How I'll Celebrate
Step 4 : Action   Due date   How I'll Celebrate

Now it's entirely possible that while you are completing these actions, you might discover new things that need to be done. Double-check your plan with the SMART goal framework. Outline any details about products or services as you understand them now. The rest you'll figure out as you create.

My MVP will be a _____ (complete a detailed description). How it works will be: _____. The resources I will need include: _____.

Entrepreneurs need a bias for action. Keep track in your startup journal of what works and doesn't. As you try things, there will be ups and downs, so keep your sense of humor and a playful attitude. Write down your game plan and add a due date. Plan to celebrate that milestone. It's important to acknowledge your efforts and success.

Building and Iterating. Describe the process to build your first offering. As you develop the concept, you'll improve incrementally, by making small improvements. Your plan should be to get it into people's hands for feedback. Creating and sustaining that urgency may require help. Support may include making an accountability partner. Put the schedule into your calendar to stay on top of your due dates.

Beta Testing – Proof of Concept. The concept of a minimum viable product is similar to a proof of concept or prototype, a popular idea in entrepreneurship. Once it's created, you want to get it into people's hands, in front of their eyeballs, or ears. Identify a small group of people for your beta testing group. These individuals can try your idea and give you an initial reaction. Do they like it? Want to use it again?

Spend the minimum amount of money to create something, then improve it several times until you're happy with it. Ask a few trusted friends to beta test it. This will be central to your work creating with constraints.

Chapter 3

Create with Constraints

Now that you have a sense of the direction your Minimum Viable Product will take, you'll want to stay on task creating, testing, improving, and getting feedback on it. Constraints are everywhere and no more so than in startups; your challenge is to keep working on your MVP despite constraints. The idea is to bring your concept to life, keeping it lean and affordable, while working relatively quickly.

Constraints come in a wide variety:

- Time and energy
- Money
- Help
- Equipment and resources
- Motivation and support

These are the walls, ceilings and corners, ceiling and floor of time, money, and energy – for now. By developing good habits, a timeline and budget can provide structure to your entrepreneurial journey. Commit to working with what you have. For creative people, boundaries can often focus them into more innovative and inspired decision-making. One question in this process is how to best keep moving forward with your goals?

Goals are wishes until you add due dates. I refer to them as lifelines (rather than deadlines, terrifying), time targets breathe life into projects.

DOI: 10.4324/9781003225140-3

Lifelines give you something to move toward. Each time you reach one – you get a shot of new energy to go to the next.

Rather than executing your ideas (also, terrifying), activate them. Bring your concept to life, change it up, remove, and add different features. Do it quickly. If it's not promising, move on.

Timelines provide structure to the entrepreneurial process so you can see if you're getting closer to your destination. There are a variety of physical and digital tools to manage time and money. It's worth investigating a few, and selecting one to two. Simple tools, used consistently, beat fancy stuff you don't use. Money management for artists means facing it without drama or confusion. Embrace transparency; look at it as just another resource. Employ the presence or lack of funds as a means to work with more creativity and resourcefulness.

Visualize and Recall Your Skills. Your memory can help use past successes right now. To shift to a positive mindset, recall something a moment you successfully managed time and money. Visualize your success, feel the bodily sensations. Bring that energy into this endeavor.

Self-care. At any point during these tasks, if you get overwhelmed, take a moment. Breathe. Acknowledge your feelings by writing them down or speaking them aloud. Practice a positive ritual, move your body, play music. Shift the energy. Then get back to progress.

Time and Money Management

(Breathe deeply, sit up big. Smile a bit. Bring uplifting emotional energy into the process.)

Time management is the first step to success in creating. Keep it simple. Dedicate regular time to work on your startup. Schedule that time on your calendar. You're worth it. Get help keeping appointments with yourself, use reminders, timers, ask allies to support you. Now stick to your calendar.

Get real with this. If you know Sundays are family days and you'll never be able to squeeze it in, don't kid yourself. It's fine. Make a reasonable schedule with enough time to actually do something (30 minutes for administrative tasks, 1–2 hours for deep creative work). Commit to several days a week for the next few months, or whatever you can do. Honor start and stop times in your schedule to avoid burn out (Figure 3.1).

Figure 3.1 Schedule Your Startup Work For Success by DeAngela Napier and Paula Landry.

Money management is the second step to success in the process of creating. You need cash to get going, but don't worry about rushing out and trying to raise money.

■ Decide what you can afford to spend (that you don't need to survive)
■ Spend only that
■ Keep general track of your spending

To that end, you could create an account inside your already-existing account (most banks will let you create a subsidiary checking or savings account inside your current account), or start an online-only checking account that's free or cheap, put your disposable budget for creating your project into it. Consistently use that account only. Make it easy.

Here are some in-depth tools and tips that may be useful in managing both time and funds.

Time

A secret to time management that nobody talks about nearly enough is energy management. Your energy gives you more time and focus. Have you ever flown through tasks and still had time to spare. Or had a day that crawled and you just couldn't get a thing done? This process is not about trying, it's about consistent actions taken to make your efforts automatic. The results come as a result. To do that, you need to manage your energy in order to get the most out of your time. Our feelings and energy are intertwined.

Overwhelm and self-doubt sap the energy of many performers, entertainers, and artistic people, so counteract that any way you can. That may be designing your schedule and sticking to it for 1 month, or selecting one thing to focus on daily. Before you start, decide exactly what you are doing. Ask yourself in a given moment if you're still doing that. When you're not sure, stop. Reset your brain. Write down exactly what to do. Make it easy and fun, white noise, uplifting music, healthy rewards, whatever motivates you.

Energy, time, money, and productivity are related because they're so intertwined. Here's a short list of popular techniques:

- Create an easy to reasonable schedule
- Do something to feel good prior to starting
- Create a ritual to begin; meditation, brief journaling, easy yoga, breathing exercises, short walk, whatever
- Select tools and techniques that feel right
- Get support
- Pick a reasonable budget that won't cause you stress
- Practice self-care – sleep, visualization, and healing techniques
- Start with the toughest thing

Enormous amounts of time are wasted on scheduling. A trick is to make fewer decisions, and stick with them, rather than constantly moving things around all the time. Many people resist a routine but creatives need it, and variety. Build the variety into your routine, whether that's wacky Wednesdays, or co-working online with a friend. Screw inspiration. Put in the work. Maybe inspiration will come, maybe it won't, but you'll be available should it stop by. In the meantime you're still making progress. Remember to reward yourself along the way.

Essential tools – Select one and use it consistently – based on your digital/ paper preferences:

- One Calendar and to-do list (paper or digital)
- One Project management app that you like and will use
- One Digital and paper folder/binder for your startup (backup the most important items)

If you're a Google, G-Suites person, start a Google folder, put in an Excel sheet that you can access everywhere, and make that the to-do list. (I call this the TA-DA list because it's exciting when a task is completed.) Then, schedule the most important things on your calendar. Color code if that makes things easier to find and see.

One Calendar and to-do list (paper or digital):

- Schedule your regular work time for making or managing
- Make your to-do list and schedule it on your calendar in one of those categories
- Schedule 90-minute creative time blocks and 30-minute administrative-time blocks
- Short end-of-day sprint for 10 minutes to cross the finish line

One Project management app that you like and will use:

- Test it out and see if it works for you
- Use it consistently
- Explore the features that will keep you moving, color coding and reminders, etc.

If you like to look in one place for everything you need, insert your to-do list into your calendar appointments, such as the example shown in Figure 3.2.

Tools. Multi-tasking is a myth. Every time you change tasks, you reset your brain. That wastes time. Do one thing for a period of time. Decide

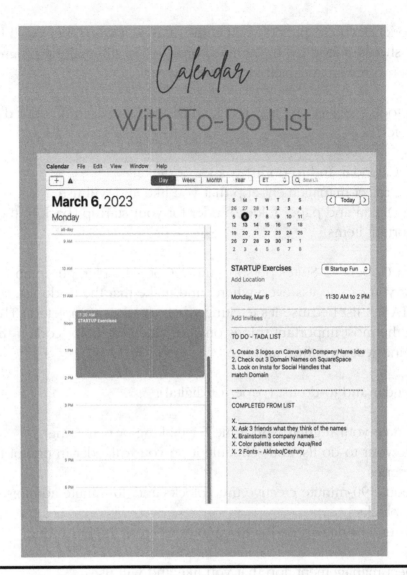

Figure 3.2 Calendar Appointment With To-Do List by DeAngela Napier and Paula Landry.

what that is before starting. Are you easily distracted? Do you chronically shop, check social media, email, or surf online? If you use the Microsoft software Word, you could try the FOCUS view, clean and simple. Block the Internet until you absolutely need it. The answers you seek are not online, they live inside you. If you need to do research, be clear about how much time you will spend online.

There are new project management tools, software, and apps all the time. Some are true project management tools to help you see and group tasks together with a timetable. Others are productivity tools. If something doesn't look appealing, skip it.

- Freedom app – a tool for blocking Internet distractions
- Trello – a visual and simple project management tool
- Asana – a project management tool
- Evernote – a note taking and storage app for multiple media
- Mindnode – a mind map tool and visual time tracker
- Focus@Will – a productivity tool using neuroscience and music
- Rescue Time – a time tracker and distraction blocker

Create an Action Plan. You have a big goal, making money by selling a great product or service. Tackling a big goal consists of dissecting it into mini-goals with actions and due dates. Just to get to the launch date where we start making money by offering our first product/service for sale, there are many steps. Observe your big goal and tackle it in smaller steps. Add actions to take specifying what to DO. Without the doing part, the action, there's no momentum, and creative people need momentum. Figure 3.3 gives one such example.

Constraints can fuel momentum. Momentum is key to creation. The easiest way to make friends with your constraints is a commitment device, like promising someone you will do something, or pairing your startup work with an activity you enjoy.

Build the Habit. It is widely thought that it takes 21 days to form a habit, so plan time intentionally, set yourself up for success by working on your startup for 21 days.

Time Chunking. Group similar activities in one time frame (10–20 minutes for email, social media, or calls). The brain likes this, you'll complete them faster since the tasks are repetitive.

Intentional and Specific Focus Periods. According to science, our brain gets about 21 minutes of focus, then we need a break. Cue the Pomodoro routine: Set aside a time chunk (25 minutes or 90 are both great). Write down what you need to do. Set the timer, do the thing. When it goes off, stop (Figure 3.4).

Healthy Rewards. Reward yourself when you do what you promised. Just like dog training, positive reinforcement works.

Maker vs. Manager Time. Use your circadian rhythms. People are more productive at certain times of the day. Schedule challenging tasks when you are most productive. Schedule maker time when you can concentrate the

Goal

Action Plan

Big Goal

Generate profits with my startup in 3 months

Mini-Goal

Sell digital product, service or experience online - by 11/1

Actions   DUE DATE

Build & Test
Send Survey to 30 people to find   8/1
marketable ideas
Create 3 prototypes   8/15
Evaluate   8/27
   Select the best
Refine with my feedback   8/30
                                                           9/5

Actions   DUE DATE

Create w/Constraints
Allocate specific extra $ for this weekly   9/15
Buy/find/borrow what need to make it   9/17
Make the thing   9/20
   Test the thing   9/29
Invite 10 beta testers to try it   10/1
Refine with feedback   10/31

Figure 3.3   Converting Your Goal Into An Action Plan by DeAngela Napier and Paula Landry.

longest and you need your creative thinking. For most people, maker time is in the morning. Manager time can be broken into shorter chunks to get administrative-type work accomplished. For most people, that's the afternoon we're more distracted, so it's better to do specific things in shorter time periods (Figure 3.5).

One Thing. Select one hard thing to accomplish first. Everything afterward seems easier.

No matter what approach you use, put that into your schedule now. With a structure of time management in place, then turn to money management.

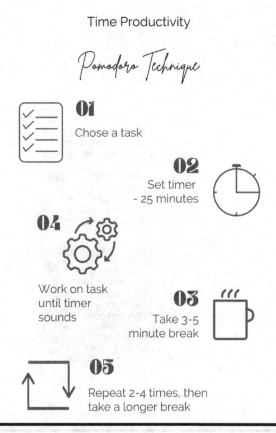

Time Productivity

Pomodoro Technique

01 Chose a task

02 Set timer - 25 minutes

04 Work on task until timer sounds

03 Take 3-5 minute break

05 Repeat 2-4 times, then take a longer break

Figure 3.4   Pomodoro Technique by DeAngela Napier and Paula Landry.

Money

Money management comes naturally to some people, and not others. There is no requirement to become a bookkeeper or an accountant to run a business. What is helpful is creating a simple system and maintaining it consistently.

During the building phase, it's necessary for entrepreneurs to apply the concept of bootstrapping, operating frugally. Don't buy if you can rent, and don't rent if you can borrow. Ask everyone for help and for freebies. (You only get away with that for a little while.) Tell them what you're doing. Frugality isn't the same thing as cheapness. Don't buy something that's shoddy if you actually need a quality tool. Borrow the high-quality tool from a colleague and return the favor.

While working on your startup, create and build budgeting habits using simple tools such as a dedicated checking account just for use as an entrepreneur. Use it consistently. There are essential money management concepts to focus on:

Figure 3.5   **Maker Versus Manager Time by DeAngela Napier and Paula Landry.**

- Decide what you can afford to spend
- Spend only that amount
- Keep track of your spending in one place
- Establish specific financial goals
- Pay yourself as soon as you can
- Select a realistic price for what you sell that's not too low
- Bootstrap as much as possible – but spend wisely
- Value your time (at a high rate, like $500/hour and up)
- When you're about to pay a high price, ask if whatever that is could bring in that $ amount in sales
- Plan for taxes (stash half of sales)
- Keep cash available for when you really need it

Allocate resources to create your MVP, make sure it's extra money that you don't need to survive. Startups are risky by nature. We don't know which product or service will yield the best results. Money is a constant constraint in the startup landscape, so this self-reliance and ingenuity that comes with this discipline will pay off in the future many times.

A fundamental step is creating how you will generate revenue, and what expenses you need in order to do so. Creating a budget for your MVP helps reveal essential expenses and figure things out as you do them.

Costs at this point should be toward creating, testing, marketing, and launching your MVP (rather than building an overall business with hiring employees, leasing office space, insurance, etc.).

Basic Budgeting

The process of building your initial budget begins by making a list of what you will create (don't worry about marketing yet).

- Raw materials
  - Who will let me borrow this?
  - Where could I rent or find this cheaply? (eBay, Amazon, Facebook Marketplace, Craigslist.)
- What type of help will I need?
  - Who will help me for free? (Free takes longer, but it's free.)
- What will the help cost? (Ask friends for recommendations, research this.)

Your Minimal Viable Product can't be so minimal that a user can't actually use it, or won't find the value.

Create your budget in your startup journal, or with a spreadsheet program.

1. Add what you need
2. Keep a list of items that are not necessary right now

Here are some things that may be on your budget:

- Basic materials, software, hardware, other equipment
- Hardware (computer monitor, headset, microphone, only necessities)
- Technical/mechanical help (if applicable)
- Creative/design help (if applicable)
- Miscellaneous services
- Total

SAMPLE

Budgets

Budget for Building your MVP	
Materials	$34
Supplies	275
Software	53
Online Service	0
Hardware	99
Legal Advice	0
Design	91
Copywriting	0
Technical Service	0
Freelancers	34
Miscellaneous	121
Legal	35
Tax Advice	9
Other	0
Total	$717

List What You Think You Need &
Stay Frugal

Figure 3.6   Sample Budget by Paula Landry.

Figure 3.6 shows a basic sample budget.

Ask friends and colleagues in similar creative fields what they did in a similar situation. Be as resourceful as possible. If you need freelance help, look on freelance platforms, like Upwork.com or Fiverr.

There is a difference between fixed costs and variable costs. Fixed costs remain the same no matter how much your business produces, like insurance and rent, web hosting, bank fees, Internet service, one-time equipment cost, or software subscriptions.

Variable costs depend on the output produced (think of products, if you are making more of something, the costs go up). Variable costs tend to fluctuate, travel, utilities, events, freelance services, and raw materials.

The goal for both is only to incur these costs when you absolutely need to and to make them the smartest expenditures possible. If you're unsure of what a specific thing should cost – do a few minutes of searching online. If you can't find that information, come back to it.

Accounting and bookkeeping relate to recording transactions and monitoring your startup's financial health. Bookkeeping involves keeping track of spending, record-keeping, and how you categorize expenses. One reason to keep track of expenses is that some will be tax deductible and could reduce the amount of income tax owed. Accounting builds on that information and helps you make plans around that. GAAP stands for "generally accepted accounting principles," and these are the standards for business accounting and money management. Taxes are based on the law, which dictates the expenses that are deductible, how income is allocated, and rules related to paying people. It's fantastic to get a bookkeeper or accountant to help you set up your accounts and books. However, you don't have to do that immediately. Figure out how to create something within your constraints and sell it. Keep track of money spent and made in one place. There are several apps that may be useful:

■ Wave – a basic small business financial app
■ Mint (by Intuit, one of the most prominent bookkeeping software companies). Intuit's software QuickBooks is popular bookkeeping software for businesses
■ Goodbudget – good for startups and freelancers and can share your budget
■ YNAB (you need a budget)

As you come to understand how you'll use your time and money, turn your creativity toward creating your business model.

Crafting Your Business Model

One of the most important things for a startup to understand is its business model. A business model has two parts:

■ Exactly how you will generate sales
■ What are your fundamental costs

Describe exactly how you will generate income including how people will pay you, and how often. Are you creating customers for life who will buy many times? Or creating a subscription model? How do you get paid? Where do they pay you – in real life or online? If online, where?

For example, suppose you're a painter selling a subscription of original paintings to hospitals to update their look seasonally. You have a detailed contract (more on this topic in Chapter 6). The Business Model: You generate sales by a company paying you to plan, sketch, design, and create original paintings. Costs include canvas, paint, brushes, design software, time, help, hanging, and shipping.

Create your business model, describe how you generate sales (what people pay you for), and what are your main costs.

The goal is to explain this information succinctly to yourself and others. Jot down what you understand so far in your startup journal.

- What will I sell and how is it unique
- Whom should I sell to
- How will they benefit
- How should customers pay
- What will major costs be for me

Consider Your Payment Process

Think of payment as two sides of a coin – the journey of your customer to pay you, and how you will get paid. You may have one way to get paid or several. Making this as secure, fast, and easy as possible, on both sides, is the goal. As the seller, no matter what you sell and how, there will be fees and costs.

Selling Online. Online ecommerce stores (eBay, Shopify, Threadless, Etsy, Wal-Mart, and Amazon platforms) with built-in ecommerce components that do everything for you. Are those platforms a good fit for your customers? Website platforms like Wix, Squarespace, and WordPress have ecommerce components for DIY. Companies like Wix allow you to design and create a site for free (without a custom domain) to see if you like how it looks and works. Creating a site yourself can be one way to see how this works.

How You Will Get Paid. There are a number of ways to get paid. Make sure yours is reliable and easy to troubleshoot. If you have an online store, compare platforms, use the tools they offer. The idea is not to waste time here, to get going as quickly as possible, but not to lose too much in fees and expenses. In payments, the goal is reliable, fast, and secure with the minimum fees.

Think about when people will pay you, one time or with a subscription service. If you're not going to use a website or online store, you may want to make sure you have PayPal, Zelle, or Cash app setup so people can pay in various ways that are convenient for them. If you sell via certain platforms, take advantage of the payment methods they already have set up.

On your side of the transaction, you will need a bank. The bank will accept payments for you, then deposit them into your account. This could be a specific merchant bank account you create just for your startup (seek out low fees) or your own bank account. Often, solo-preneur startups will use their own accounts at first.

On the other side of the transaction, is your customer with a credit or debit card (the issuing bank). They will need to communicate.

Technologies between you and your customer include:

■ A payment gateway (software linking your website's shopping cart to a payment processing network)
■ A payment processor (also known as merchant service). If your merchant bank is also your payment processor, then that simplifies matters

Payment processing includes authorization (sale approval) and settlement (moving money into your account).

The authorization process:

1. Your customer buys an item on your site with a credit or debit card
2. That information goes through the payment gateway, encrypting data to keep it private, and sends it to the payment processor
3. The payment processor sends a request to the customer's issuing bank to check to see that they have enough credit to pay
4. The issuer responds with approval or denial
5. The payment processor sends that info to you. If approved it tells your merchant bank to credit your account for the money

Payment settlement (you get paid):

a. The card issuer sends funds to your bank, depositing them into your account
b. The funds are available

The settlement process isn't always instantaneous.

Payment involves fees. These entities will each take a percent of the sale:

6. Payment issuing bank

7. The credit card association (Visa, MasterCard, etc.)
8. Your accepting merchant bank
9. The payment processor/online store

Fees will range from 3% to 10% per sale; it's the cost of doing business. More robust platforms (which charge more) have better customer service.

How Will People Pay. Think of the transactions in your life that are difficult and why. Whether it's too many steps, or lost passwords, or you're not sure if the transaction is secure, this information can help you design a customer payment experience that is as friendly as possible.

Once in your ecommerce store, the customer might click on wares in your store and add them to the cart. They may create an account (or not – guest checkout). When a client buys something they must enter certain information, email, name, address components, phone number sometimes, payment information such as credit card or debit numbers (name, card number, Security code – CVV, as well as the expiration date of the payment card, address). If the person uses PayPal or something similar and you have that enabled, maybe they can just log into their PayPal and pay with fewer clicks.

Our job as retailers online is to make this process as secure, quick, and seamless as possible. An important part of your selling process is checkout, as this converts into revenue. Checkout is the step that is abandoned most frequently. You may not have control over every aspect of the payment process. So don't sweat it. Fix what you can control, get help when necessary.

Once you've built a platform to buy, test out the payment experience several times, on varying devices in different web browsers and on a Smartphone.

In your startup journal, do a bit of research and decide:

- Where is the best destination to sell my offering
- What do I need to start that process

Find Partners

Finding partners during the creating process can offer accountability, emotional support, and advice. Select one or more to aid you to stay on track and inspired. Human commitment devices come in a few different categories.

Accountability Partners. Choose one or two accountability partners – not for forever – just for a while. Ask them to help you stay on your path by checking in weekly. These may be close friends, or a pesky aunt who's very self-disciplined, or a colleague who's also striving to improve herself and grow. You will help the other person as you help yourself.

Cheerleader. Another great type of partner is a cheerleader who will support your goals and journey and wants you to succeed. Engage them in your process for positive feedback. This should be a different person than your accountability partner, ideally.

Big Dogs. If there is someone you admire, whether a colleague in your industry, mentor, former partner, or professor, and you are in contact with them, sharing your work with them may help you.

Business Partner. If you're seeking an ongoing business partner, it's possible to find one, but there may be pitfalls. Partners may lead to groupthink, and democracy rather than realizing YOUR true vision. I'm not discouraging you from seeking business partners, but choose carefully if you really need one.

Defining and Locating Your Customers and Audience

Who your people are, and where they can be found, is something that you need to constantly ask yourself. Once you find them, try to get in their heads, get feedback from them. Ask yourself, what does this person want, like, and need.

Sending surveys out is one way to get feedback from potential customers. Are you having trouble locating them? Maybe you haven't defined them to an extent you find them in the first place. Creating a buyer persona is helpful, because you have to get specific. This is an example of one customer persona, representing an ideal customer (Table 3.1).

This may be overly detailed, but describe as much as you do know. In your startup journal, create a buyer persona for your ideal fan, follower, audience, client, customer, subscriber – whatever you call this person. If you have more than one persona for your buyer, create each individually. Initially, you want to search for those that you think of as early adopters, the people who will try, and buy your offering right away.

Now you have a detailed sense of your buyers. Where are they?

Start searching online for them. Use key words from your persona, describing her, her interests. Seek out groups online, via social media, meet-ups, trade organizations, and the various activities she might participate in. Use several different terms for these hobbies and activities. For

Table 3.1 Buyer Persona

Persona	College Nina
Description	19 years old Sophomore undergraduate at Wamswow College outside of New York City Studying to work in social media marketing Grew up in a medium-sized city Wants to live/work in big city
Profile	• Driven and ambitious, high energy • Lives on her phone • Creates "marketing" activity for her ferret on socials • Organized, does everything ahead of time • Wears many hats at her part time marketing internship • Plays sports like rugby, basketball, and water polo • Single, seeking love • Comedy and music lover who lives on Spotify, TikTok, IG • Fashionista on a budget • Loves comedy and binge-watches YouTube for funny people • Outgoing. Trend and culture conscious • Devoted to family and friends • Daring, will try anything once

example – filmmakers call themselves film producers, film directors, movie makers, cinephiles, content creators, and a variety of other terms. By searching on Google (because they own Internet search) find the correct terminology to seek out WHERE your customer hangs out online and in real life.

In your startup journal, note where these communities can be found. This will help you connect with them, through these organizations and platforms in your marketing.

Then look at your own connections:

■ Social media
■ Your contacts
■ Friends and family
■ Friends of friends and family
■ Folks from outside your work life, neighbors, church, kids sports teams, book club, alumni, other groups, and your past

In your startup journal, create a list of who may be able to help you make contact with your tribe. Let them know what you're up to. Ask if they can help you get in touch with people who may be interested in what you're doing. Once you start finding these prospective customers ("prospects") create a simple survey. In the survey, ask specific questions about your MVP idea – Does the idea sound attractive? Would they buy it? For what price point? What other ideas do they have about this?

As you cultivate these relationships, it can be helpful to organize the information. There are a variety of ways to do this. Keeping track of patron information is called CRM, customer relationship management.

Organizing Customers and Fans with CRM (Customer Relationship Management)

CRM stands for Customer Relationship Management. It means keeping track of your customers. It's common to track name and email at the minimum. If you are selling a product, you may have an address for them, and some people like to track how they met. CRM software tools can track buying information, customer segment, or activity in your sales funnel, such as emails opened, actions taken, and so forth. Initially, a spreadsheet program would work to organize the information rather than, or in addition to, a CRM program.

Mini Case Study. Entrepreneur and Music Executive Walter J. Tucker, MBA, founded a business in New York City based on networking and professional music–education events called LiveThe.Biz. Events included aspiring professional musicians as well as accomplished performers and professionals. They grew over time in popularity, consisting of fun, high-quality educational and networking components. Mr. Tucker went on to become a successful music executive, thought-leader, and college professor as well as entrepreneur, maintaining and growing events for a widespread population in several locations. Speaking at a seminar for graduate MBA students, Walter shared that one key to his success was his personalized and detailed approach to networking. He related how he organized and made notes on the professionals he met, with a brief description of when, where, and an interesting personal factoid about them. The personal detail might be a mutual enjoyment of Marvel movies, favorite music genre, even something anecdotal. This helped him reconnect on a personal level with that individual again in the future. This connection allowed him to build on the relationship. You can follow him at @livethebiz on Instagram.

Spreadsheets, contact programs in your computer, phone, and email, can be used for this purpose. There are also many software tools you could use such as Constant Contact, Zoho, Hubspot, FreeCRM, Mailchimp, or others. The benefit of using robust tools like these is that you can segment them into different customer categories if that's relevant. For example, you may want to market to a particular demographic in a certain age range. If you gather that information, you can separate your email list that way. (If you don't track that information, you cannot, obviously.)

Robust CRM software records customer details, documents interactions, and keeps it in one place. You can analyze the information to learn if your efforts are effective. CRM can be simple or can go deep. Ideally, the right system will help you manage your customers, win you more new ones, and make your current customers happy.

You don't need a CRM system right away, but it is a powerful tool for growth. No matter your approach to your customers, or the overall creation process, keep a sense of urgency. This is different than stress. Translate urgency into excitement to create this for you, your growth, and your future (Figure 3.7).

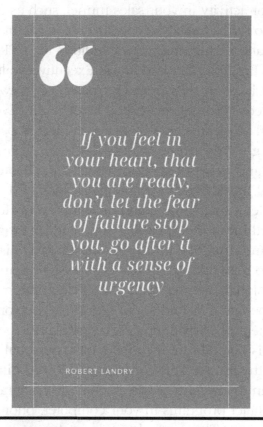

> *If you feel in your heart, that you are ready, don't let the fear of failure stop you, go after it with a sense of urgency*
>
> ROBERT LANDRY

Figure 3.7   Quote by Robert Landry.

As a conclusion, your MVP will progress as you stay on task creating, testing, improving, and getting feedback on it. Constraints require creativity, which you definitely have. At some point, you will need to declare your MVP as "finished" even if it's imperfect. Keep a firm date by which you will share your work with the public. Crafting the messages around sharing, and building your brands, will build excitement for you and help you transmit that to the world.

Chapter 4

Share with Awareness

Once you've built something, you need to share it with fans. Start with
a select and trusted group of beta fans. How you share, the cadence,
messaging, and actions will be different for every entrepreneur. The more
you can connect with your tribe, the more in-tune your marketing will be.
Sharing the news about your startup, your entrepreneurial journey, and the
first offering is exciting. Being aware of the reactions to your marketing is
one way to make sure you're on the right track.

What is sharing with awareness?

- Understanding, recognizing, and communicating the value of what
  you sell
- Defining how you, and your offering, are unique
- Finding the people who want to find you
- Crafting how to share the information in an organic way
- Staying open to what works and what needs improvement

Much of the startup community focuses on a problem and solution
framework. This way of thinking can be helpful or detrimental. When you're
writing music, painting art, designing pottery, jewelry, or furniture, it's not
necessarily about a problem. Many disciplines are built around creating an
emotional connection to the work. Aesthetics play a strong role in many
purchases. People watch, consume, buy, and subscribe to things that they
need and love. In this case, the problem is more like offering value for
fulfillment. Shape your marketing around ideas that make sense to you.

DOI: 10.4324/9781003225140-4

Keep in touch with a small and trustworthy community that can give you constructive feedback, that is, your beta testers.

Beta Testing

Sharing with awareness is marketing with your true feelings, excitement, keeping an eye on what your fans want. Select a small group of beta testers and invite them to join you on this journey. Invite their opinions about your MVP.

In your startup journal, identify these people. Then compose and send a brief invitation to them, explaining what you will ask of them, and why.

Toss aside worries about tacky and annoying sales techniques. Artists, entertainers, performers, and creative people, when they're coming from an authentic place, should discuss their work. Sharing what you've made, and its value, is marketing. Awareness is part of the process, this isn't a one-way street. Be aware of what your buyers think, feel, their needs, desires, and wishes. The more you hear from them, the more you'll understand what they want. The digital world offers these tools, so take advantage of them.

Visualize and Recall Your Skills. At some point (maybe recently), you shared a new artist, service, or product you discovered and were enthusiastic about it. That's effective marketing. Your excitement and the feelings around that memory can fuel these activities.

If you feel self-doubt or become overwhelmed, stop and breathe. Acknowledge your feelings. Remind yourself why you're doing this. Begin again, taking one intentional step at a time.

Asking a customer you just met to purchase something they've never heard of is like proposing on a first date. It makes more sense to create awareness with your buyer, cultivate interest, and establish trust.

A marketing funnel, also called a sales funnel, is a graphical representation of your customer's journey from "I have no idea who you are, or what you're selling" to the actual sale fulfillment. This communication flow will add context to the information discussed here. Keep your potential funnel in your mind's eye, or draw some version of it and notate items on it along the way.

Marketing (Funnel)

The marketing or sales funnel illustrates the journey toward you and your offering. This process and activities build a relationship with your potential customer toward and through buying your offering. Why the sales funnel is great:

- Offers a graphic overview
- Shows your actions
- Shows the purpose of your action
- Illustrates how to move a relationship toward a sale

The process goes from basic awareness to a more detailed understanding of how your offering can benefit a buyer. From awareness to interest, with details about functionality, costs, samples, and evaluation – to "this sounds great, I'm ready to buy" and then beyond that to "I'm so happy about this, I'll share it with friends." While it's not impossible for someone to buy what you're selling in the first encounter, it's unlikely. You don't want to rely on chance. It's better to increase your odds by building clear pathways to a sale.

In the language of marketing, there are prospects (prospective customers) and leads (customers you have specifically identified). You don't have to use any specific marketing language, but you should comprehend it when you encounter these terms. The end goal is to make the process work for you.

There are a few different descriptions of the funnel segments, and they all point to the same goal – capturing the attention of a potential customer and converting that to a sale.

AIDA

AIDA stands for Attention – Interest – Desire – Action, the structure of the funnel. First, draw attention, then the customer receives more information to get interested, desiring what you're selling until; they ultimately act, that is, buying your product or service. Afterward, if they are happy, they may share with others (promotional help for you) and become repeat customers.

One goal is to move prospects through the funnel, however, it may be more layered depending on what you do. An ultimate goal may be to build a more long-term relationship with buyers and a community that's interactive, loyal, and engaged. The kind where you have the attention of a group of people you connect with and can harness that power when the time is right.

If you are building a following on a social platform or membership site, the process is the same, except that the action may be a subscription, or like, share, comment, or something similar. Certain artists, performers, and creatives may plan to create an MVP of an engaged online community,

Funnel

For Marketing & Sales

Awareness
↓
Interest
↓
Desire
↓
Action
↓
Loyalty

Stages You Take Your Customer Through
As They Purchase Your Product/Service

Figure 4.1   Sales Funnel by DeAngela Napier and Paula Landry.

perhaps on a pre-existing social media platform or their own website. The plan may be to leverage that following to sell ads, gain sponsors, wield influence. Figure 4.1 shows a multi-stage sales funnel based on a version of AIDA.

Any of these might be included at various parts of the funnel:

Awareness
- Online and search ads
- Videos
- Animated gifs
- Social media content
- Social media ads
- SEO
- Website
- eBooks
- LinkedIn outreach
- Blog and vlog (video blogging)

    – Contests/games/quizzes/polls
    – Assessments/questionnaires
    – Charts/graphs
    – Teaching/speaking
    – Guest on media, TV, radio, podcasts, blogs
    – Press release

Interest
    – Case studies/white papers
    – Infographics
    – Email campaigns and direct mail newsletters
    – Events/webinars/meet ups/classes
    – Calculators (if applicable)
    – Interactive eBooks
    – Wizards (if applicable)
    – Trade shows/demos
    – Guest collaborations
    – Streaming events
    – Animated charts/graphs
    – Presentation/speaking at industry events
    – Live readings/performances/showcases
    – Art fairs/public exhibitions

Desire
    – Chat bots
    – Phone conversations
    – Email
    – Trial period
    – Promotional and free samples
    – Testimonials/customer reviews
    – Stars, likes, third party certifications
    – Personalized demonstrations

Action
    – Sale
    – Buy
    – Subscribe
    – For platform building – like, follow, share, comment, free subscription
    – Loyalty

- Renew subscriptions
- Referring
- Surveys
- Write reviews and testimonials
- Share, like, and engage on social media
- Gift your offering to another
- Donate
- Rewards for returning browsing customers
- Rewards for returning buying customers
- Rewards for referrals

There's no reason to use all, or most, of these. Select what feels right.

Grab your startup journal and create your sales funnel, adding a few tactics to each segment.

Pitching and Storytelling

All marketing is storytelling; the best narrators win the most business. The story is reinforced in the name of a product, with a brand's origin story, and promotional activities. The most successful brands are the best storytellers, from Coke to Nike, Crayola to Apple.

Think about what you buy and the stories attached to those purchases. The story may be related to how the item or service makes you feel, appear, or behave.

Your approach to marketing should be through a framework of storytelling directed at one, specific person. Someone you really like and are letting in on this awesome experience or opportunity. Remember the juiciest story a friend even relayed, and how it felt? Conspiratorial, almost like a secret being revealed, only for you. Channel that, that sense of discovery, unearthing treasure is part of the appeal of stories. They connect us, teach us, and definitely sell us. Look at some of the ads and marketing of the brands you adore and pay attention to the stories they tell you – often placing you right in the middle of the narrative, if you'll buy and use this specific service or product.

Storytelling usually places your customer as the heroine of the movie of their lives, where they are using your product or service, with how it will make them feel and how it improves their life. While you're painting that picture, you may offer valuable information on the way. Not every communication can be about sales. We use content marketing, stories, and material to interest our customers – whether a funny video, factoid, news item, infographics, teaching tip, sharing relevant data, highlighting members in their community, or otherwise – these won't all be pitching.

The pitch is the story of how your offering (what you sell and why it's great) enhances that persons' life. The simpler, the better. A pitch asks your potential fan to do or buy something from you with a very clear Call to Action (Buy Now, Subscribe, Share). When possible, there should be a sense of urgency. Create your pitch.

My name is _____, and my product/service _____ will add _____ to your life by _____, _____ and _____. Click here to purchase, this promotion ends at midnight.

Stories are tribal, memorable, and carry emotion in them, which is why they're effective. Think of all of your marketing interactions as potential storytelling opportunities.

Build Awareness

Cultivating and building awareness are a mindset. If people don't know that you are selling something they have no way of buying it. Going back to the sales funnel, this is the start of you planting many seeds about your company in the world, and some growing. This requires you have an offering to sell, connect with who you're selling it to, and how they'll benefit. Keep an open mind because it's not always clear what messaging works best. Keep a sense of play and experimentation. Don't overspend in marketing.

Once you have defined your brand, building awareness is typically comprised of content marketing and will:

■ Define features and benefits
■ Share benefits first
■ Stay open to what your customers want
■ Market to a specific customer
■ Get social proof (testimonials, reviews), whenever possible

An important aspect of sharing your products and services is learning how to answer questions from people interested in buying your offering. As an entrepreneur you must continuously define and seek out your fan base (your buyers), create a strategy and brand for various offerings (what you sell), plan your promotional activities (marketing and sharing), then activate your plan (do the steps you've outlined). Afterward, it's important to review what happened to improve the process going forward. This isn't linear, it's actually circular. Ongoing relationships between you and your customer will tend to deepen as time goes on. Your attitude is that anyone who becomes a fan or follower keeps coming back. This gives you the opportunity to grow the bond (Figure 4.2).

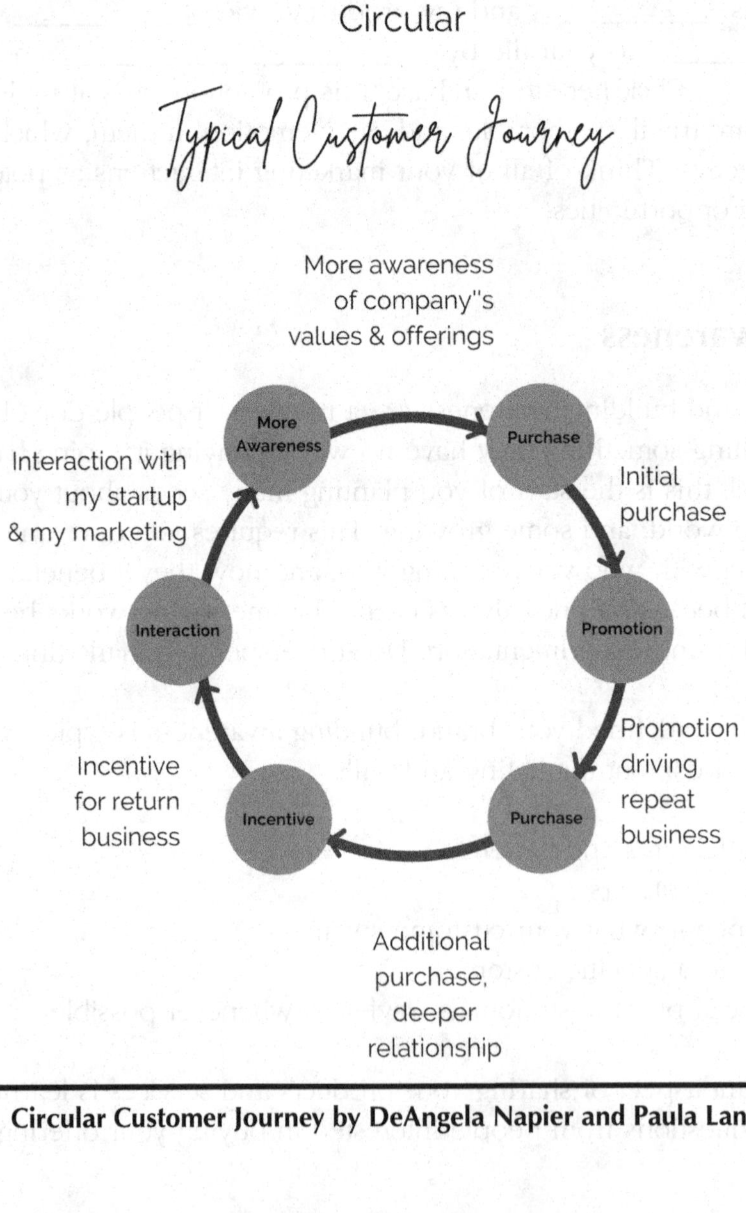

Figure 4.2   Circular Customer Journey by DeAngela Napier and Paula Landry.

Branding

Your brand stands for the promise you make to your audience. It is a visual representation of your startup identity, reinforced with your messaging and graphical cues.

These are the building blocks of a brand:

- Logo
- Colors in your marketing and image
- Types of images
- Types of messaging used in marketing
- Tagline
- Unique value proposition of your product or service
- Mission statement
- Bio of you (or a persona you create) with a startup story (the reason I started this...)
- The tone of your communications
- Social proof (reviews and testimonials)

You may include something you're known for. Creative people often capitalize on some recognizable trait, and it becomes something they're known for. This may be a manner of dressing or style. It may be something you already do and it's so innate that you don't even notice it. Consider asking a couple of close friends and colleagues about this – if there's something they always think of when they think of you – and consider whether that could be incorporated into your actual branding.

Branding takes time, meshing the values you ascribe to your work and the values that your audience experiences, and accepts. New brands have little brand equity or recognition with people because they're unknown. Every time you sell something or interact with a customer in any way, it will reinforce or deny the brand you're creating.

Visualize and Recall Your Skills. You're skilled at identifying branding messages. You've been exposed to brands throughout your entire lifetime. Recognizing logos and what they stand for is a skill that you may not think about often. Bring that skill with you throughout the creation and honing of your brand.

Before you spend a ton of time and energy on creating a brand you need to know who else is in the same space as you are. It's important to understand who else sells what you do and to make sure you don't confuse your customers. You can do this with a bit of market research. Also, if you want to articulate your brand in comparison to others, create a SWOT analysis.

Conducting a SWOT and Market Research. In the startup world, companies often perform market research. This saves time. Also, research helps ensure that you're not missing something obvious in the marketplace. The process can shine a light on a sustainable niche in your market. Creating a SWOT analysis is one way to compare your startup to competitors, with a systematic approach to Strengths and Weaknesses, Opportunities and Threats. If you're an analytical person, create a SWOT for your startup. Figure 4.3 shows the format of a SWOT.

Grab your startup journal. Answer relevant questions that apply to your startup to complete a SWOT analysis.

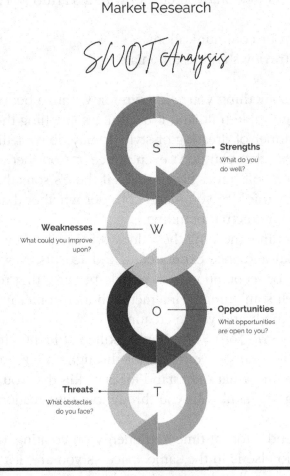

Market Research

SWOT Analysis

S ———• **Strengths**
What do you do well?

Weaknesses •——— W
What could you improve upon?

O ———• **Opportunities**
What opportunities are open to you?

Threats •——— T
What obstacles do you face?

Figure 4.3 SWOT by DeAngela Napier and Paula Landry.

Strengths: What advantages does your startup have, and what do you do to better others? What unique (differentiated) attributes do you have? What factors could clinch your sale? What resources are easily available to you? What relationships can help you?

Weaknesses: What do competitors do better than you do? What could you improve upon? What are people in your market (customers or competitors) likely to perceive as weaknesses? What factors might drive customers to choose competitors over you?

Opportunities: Where are these opportunities/openings available for you? Are there trends or opportunities you could use to your advantage, such as changes in market needs, laws, regulations, technology, social patterns and behaviors, population profiles, lifestyle changes, and local environments?

Threats: What obstacles do you face? Are specifications relating to your products or services changing? Is changing technology a potential problem?

With an understanding of where your Minimum Viable Product is compared to similar products or services, craft and define your brand.

Market research jumpstarts the branding process, to find direct and indirect competitors, and understand price points. You don't need to craft your brand as an alternative to every other competitor out there, but you don't want to copy them, either. Spend 10–20 minutes to research what other people or companies are doing, what you are looking at in their website and social platforms to pinpoint where your offering is similar or different, and who they're marketing to.

In your startup journal, define your brand:

1. Select vivid words from your mission statement and value proposition. By selecting various traits you want to be associated with your brand early, you can use them to keep your brand on track. In the long run, it might mean staying transparent, not using certain materials or language, treating people in a certain way
2. Think of a few brands you admire
3. Select a company name to represent you, what you're selling, what you do, or some combination. Make sure nobody else is using it for the same type of business
4. Select web domain and social handles (make sure they're available)
5. Select colors
6. Create a logo – test on others. The best logos tend to be simple. Color-wise, the logo should be planned with the Internet in mind, and you

will need a black and white version. Create a version just as a graphic – and one with your company name. Until you have established your identity you will need to have the symbol and name connected

7. Select two fonts – one main and one secondary
8. Create your branded email signature
9. Write a tiny bio about you and your business
10. Create a tagline if you want one – test on others. Taglines often help to explain what a business does
11. Share feedback from people you trust
12. Define the personality of your brand
13. Briefly define the tone of communications from your brand (how does it talk?)
14. Position your brand – How are you different from other brands (or people if there aren't any) in this space – plucky underdog, luxury, aloof, friendly, value, etc.
15. Your UVP and mission statement are important components of your brand
16. How does your Minimum Viable Product embody or reflect your brand

This can change down the line, but for now you have something to move forward with and use in all your promotional activities. Once you have designed your brand use it consistently across all communications. Over time you will create brand equity, which is the association of your brand with values and performance.

Logo resources include Canva, 99 Designs, and online freelance marketplaces to hire designers.

Slogan makers resources:

■ https://www.shopify.com/tools/slogan-maker?itcat=blog&itterm=215822345
■ https://www.designhill.com/tools/slogan-maker
■ https://snazzy.ai/
■ https://www.oberlo.com/tools/slogan-generator

If you're stuck on a name, take the time to ask friends, family, and potential customers about the name and see if they like it, associate it with what you're selling. Make sure the name of your startup doesn't clash with what you're offering for sale. Initially you can function as a DBA (doing business as), which means that you personally are the company, rather than spending time and money to legally incorporate (more on this in Chapter 6). One reason to wait on forming a company is that you may not yet know what structure you want to form, and rushing into forming a legal structure can be complex and has implications for taxes that you will owe. Naming resources:

■ https://businessnamegenerator.com/
■ https://www.shopify.com/tools/business-name-generator/
■ https://howtostartanllc.com/business-name-generator
■ https://namelix.com/

Marketing Fundamentals: The 4Ps or SIVA

The marketing mix (also known as the "The 4Ps") is a framework for the various activities to create and build awareness with your target audience. The 4Ps is a traditional approach, whereas SIVA is more of a value-centric, community-building model. Look at the brief overview of each before selecting one to use.

The 4Ps include defining your:

■ Product, service, or experience – what you're selling
■ Price – how much it costs
■ Place – where/how people buy it
■ Promotion – activities to build awareness about what you're selling (Figure 4.4)

Product/Service/Experience. Concisely and vividly articulate what you are selling, your product, service, or experience; succinctly convey the value it offers to buyers and how it's unique. Include the benefits and features. If you're selling something meant to solve a problem, highlight the needs they can fulfill for the problems they can solve.

Pricing can be based on research on similar offerings (position above or below, but don't underprice) or based on your expenses. If it costs you $X to make something, multiply that by three or four for your price. Pricing is an art and a science. Become aware of prevailing prices for similar offerings. You may want to price your offering in relation to them – positioning yourself as a sassy and affordable upstart, or perhaps the luxury choice such as an aspirational selection which calls for higher prices.

The 4 P's

Marketing Mix

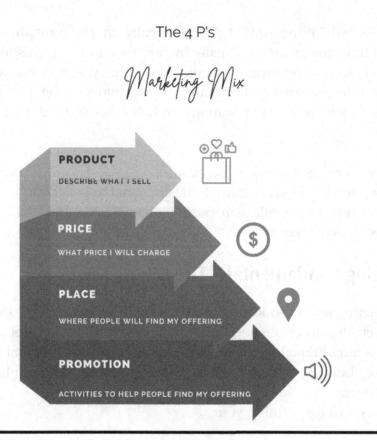

Figure 4.4   The 4 P's by DeAngela Napier and Paula Landry.

When you present your prices for multiple items to your fans, present the higher price first – you can always go down. When people see the next price that's lower than the first, it will feel like a bargain.

There's a point at which you're charging too little or too much and that has to be finessed, often through trial and error. Beware of the rock-bottom mentality, you can always have a sale or promotion for a limited period of time. If you sell a tangible item that must be shipped – calculate the shipping and handling and factor that into your price. Pricing strategies abound, $19.99 versus $20, some swear that prices that end in the numeral 5 cause more sales. There are many different approaches to pricing:

■ Skimming: if you're the first to market, you could charge a high price to maximize profits. Disadvantage: High profits attract competition
■ Market penetration: The company could start with low prices to grab market share and keep competitors out. Disadvantage: Profit margins will be lower

- Cost-based pricing: Your cost plus a mark-up
- Demand-based pricing: Price based on what customers will pay (look at competition)

Place or placement is where people buy or consume. The "place" might be online on your website or Facebook marketplace, Etsy or some other Internet store, on Vimeo, YouTube, or Zoom. Or the place may be some geographic area, in a real-world store, art festival, gallery, or other. One reason to understand the "where" of your customers is maximizing any money you spend to reach them with your marketing. If you boost a post or buy an ad online – there's no point in paying for a gigantic geographic area if customers must be near or in New York City in order to buy your offering. When you are online, you are essentially worldwide, but you must focus your marketing efforts on the locations where most of your customers are in order to maximize your efforts.

Promotion activities are where we'll spend most of our time and make up the entire Marketing Funnel. They consist of the assorted actions you take to help the people who should find you – discover what you're doing. These are the things at the top of your funnel – generating awareness and trying to spur interest. Whether this is blogging, newsletters, social media posting and ads, events, or other tactics, some experimentation may be necessary at the beginning. In this context, this promotional plan you create consists of all the things you're going to do to attract your customer's attraction. That's different than running a promotion, like a sale or discount or give away, of course you can do these as well, however, these are more like incentives. Promotion should be a robust plan for what and how you'll communicate the value of your offerings.

Even if you have Etsy, Amazon, eBay, Shopify, or other ecommerce stores, build a simple website. This is a destination that people can easily find, see what is for sale, get your social links, sign up for your newsletter and contact you.

Marketing activities can spur overwhelm. Keep it focused. Allocate regular time for promotions. Don't manage too many platforms. Do things that are fun for you. Select three to four methods and be consistent for a while to see what is effective.

SIVA. The difference between the 4Ps and SIVA is that SIVA is more service oriented and experientially focused (Figure 4.5).

- Think of your product as a solution (or sensation)
- Share information about what you're selling (rather than promotions)

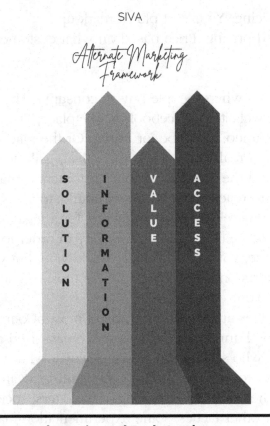

Figure 4.5 SIVA by DeAngela Napier and Paula Landry.

- Give value in exchange for payment (instead of price)
- How do customers access your offer (contrasting with placement)

Solution/Sensation: This flips the script from what entrepreneurs want to sell to – what does our customer desire, need, or wish for. For performers, entertainers, and creatives, you could apply this by defining your offering as a Solution, or delivering a Sensation that the person will benefit from, and getting specific about that, whether delight, enchantment or wonder, convenience, speed, or an improvement in their life.

An Example: Here's an example of the SIVA model utilized in marketing a product with variety and an authentic voice. The CEO of the company Cat Doodles pitched to the television show Shark Tank. Shark Tank features seasoned investors who hear pitches then decide whether or not to invest in the business, explaining why on the show. The entrepreneur's business was a service, creating simple and humorous drawings of cats as requested by clients. He included rapping, music, a sense of fun, and humor. He posted drawings requested by customers on his website, making a thousand drawings in a week. He sold 1,200 cat pictures in 3 years, and the sensation of fun and personalization are evident at his website: https://iwanttodrawacatforyou.com. The promotion on the television show provided fun information about his services and access was clearly through his website. Not every entrepreneur will be on a television show, however, the approach may give you some fun ideas about how to customize SIVA for your startup.

Rather than a promotional mindset, "look here and buy this," providing information is an approach of generosity and fulfillment of curiosity. To apply this, showcase benefits to customers, provide social proof like reviews or testimonials. It's about developing a relationship, with engagement, that leads to sales. Sharing information that will help your tribe, whether it garners sales or not, is important. Pay attention to the social media accounts you follow and why, dissecting what aspect of their messages appeals to you. This will help you shape your own strategy. The online search process is a very real way of how people will find you, so you need to give them solid information along their search.

The SIVA model flips Price to Value. Posing the question "What is the value I'm providing to my customers" helps you figure this out. To apply this, research what others with comparable offerings are charging. Many content creators sell intangible products that cannot be priced based on raw materials, so the pricing process can be tricky. Value to customers may be heightened by the speed of delivery of your offering, convenience and ease of use, fun and aesthetics that you deliver. Querying customers about pricing can be very helpful when determining the value of your offering.

Customers always want things right away, so Access replaces Place. The reason that is important is the digital sphere will be how and where customers access your experiences, services, and products. That means that your offering is available 24/7, 365 days a year, worldwide. To apply this, craft the customer's process to access your offering in a way that is seamless, enjoyable, and as easy as possible. Because services are often not designed to immediately fill a need or solve a problem, your emphasis should be more on establishing a relationship with the potential customer.

One overall goal is to keep variety in your marketing and convey an authentic voice. Those that are successful, like the following example, can find success in a fun and genuine way.

Mini Case Study. Charles Chessler is a professional photographer in New York City and a man of many talents. Embarking upon a photography career, he utilized strategic giving, by offering free images to his photography subjects, as a way to learn. In New York, there are many actors, and they need updates on headshots regularly. Charlie began doing headshots for actors, using Facebook to share the best images (with permission) which attracted more attention and clients. This organic approach to marketing built word-of-mouth and an outstanding reputation. As his skills improved, he leveled up on equipment and began sharing his talents with organizations, often for free. Some of which went on to hire him. He shared his talents with others by teaching, doing photo walks in Manhattan parks, as well as with organizations like B&H which sell photography equipment. Mr. Chessler is quick to recognize an opportunity to capture great images and build both skills and relationships. A fan of musical artist Emily McDuff, he photographed her regularly at her shows, and that relationship grew in ways which expanded his knowledge and skills. Charles was invited to shoot images at one of Emily's recording sessions with famous studio musicians in Nashville, a setting that is very intimate and private. It yielded wonderful pictures, while growing his skills and relationships. Charles is passionate about photography and unabashed in his quest to improve, with a vulnerability and enthusiasm, which is contagious. He jumped at the opportunity to photograph a rhinoceros dehorning in South Africa. He is now leading photography safaris as a result, and sharing images of rhino dehorning that can save their species and doesn't harm them. The combination of generosity and enthusiasm is enticing, no matter whether Charles offers his services shooting portraits or headshots, teaching, collaborating, or more. See his work and learn more at www.charleschesslerphotography.com.

Now, using either framework, complete The 4Ps or SIVA as it pertains to your startup.

Sales

The key to sales is marketing your product in a focused manner, using different channels with an authentic voice. Whether you're using social media, text, or email marketing, or something else, strive for consistency and clarity.

Messaging and copywriting are important aspects of sales. In all of your copy, write to one person and emphasize the benefits of your offering. Use stories and use a call to action. Don't be afraid, in a direct setting, to ask for a sale when the opportunity arises. People instinctively know when they are being sold to and often avoid it. Finding the right balance of communications, which are generous with information, build trust, help your community, share opportunities that can help when you are selling directly.

If you have met a natural salesperson, it's easy to admire that innate-seeming gift. But the energy and persistence you used to create your MVP can be used here. If you need to, construct a separate persona (wear a perky hat, maybe). Whatever helps. Remember you are sharing value with the world and your customers need to find you. Keep your confidence and optimism and remember it's about finding the fans who want to find you and your offering.

Features versus Benefits. In the sales and promotional process, emphasize the benefits of your service, product, or experience. A feature is something that your product has or is. That feature may make it more attractive, efficient, faster, or more convenient. Benefits are how your customer receives satisfaction from your MVP, they may be physical, emotional, or a sensation.

Benefits are the outcomes or results that users will (hopefully) experience by using your product or service – the very reason why a prospective customer becomes an actual customer.

Example. A designer has decided to do a cellphone case as an MVP. This offering is something new for her customers. She's an ardent environmentalist, whose customers tend to be Gen Z folks (primarily women) in college or just out of college, and women over 45 who are passionate about helping the planet. Table 4.1 lists the features and benefits of new cellphone cases.

From your interactions with your beta users and through your survey tools, what seem to be the most important benefits? If you don't know, then it's time to talk to your people so that you can lead with those benefits. Understand that it's possible what you think are the most important benefits may be different from what your audience, users, and fans really prefer. That's part of the overall discovery in launching your startup.

Table 4.2 gives an example of the most important benefits the designer discovered in a survey from fans.

Ask your beta testers – what are the most important benefits of your offering?

Content Marketing

Content marketing is the overall term for the majority of marketing we see online; blogs, social media, and email newsletters all offer the opportunity for you to share with your audience. The content you create for your

Table 4.1 Features and Benefits

Features	Benefits
The phone cases we design and sell are flashy	Easy to see and read
	Easy to find (hard to lose)
	Looks cool (noticeable by others)
The phone cases we design and sell are customizable	Make a personal gift and can be quirky
	One of a kind – unique gift
	Sparks conversations by strangers
The phone cases we design and sell are made from environmentally friendly material	Doesn't harm the earth – makes customers feel good about less waste, eco-smarts
	Dissolves in 1 year – with flower seeds in the paper to actually grow a plant, helping the planet
	Flower seeds are those that attract bees, so helps endangered bees when discarded

Table 4.2 Key Benefits

Benefits
One of a kind – unique gift, nobody else has
Flower seeds in the case are those that attract bees, so helps endangered bees when discarded
Doesn't harm the earth – makes customers feel good about less waste, eco-smarts

audience will vary depending on your bandwidth – how much time and energy you put into this. Allocate a specific strategy and regular time to do content marketing; include news, education, promotional posts, contests, influencer posts, events, Q&A, behind-the-scene images, music, memes, and testimonials. Some of the best engagement can come by sharing the content of others. Remember that video is one of the most dominant attractors in marketing, trending toward mobile content.

With practice, you will learn to convey your values and vision of your content. Collect examples that you like, from social content to web pages to email newsletters. Keep them in your startup files with notes about what to use.

Design is of growing importance in every aspect of marketing. There are many resources on design. Evaluate why you are drawn to something visually. Most people gravitate to contrast and balance. Remember to give your viewer's eyes variety, movement, hierarchy, proportion, repetition, and patterns. Seek comprehension and ease over anything too fancy. Whose design would you like to emulate in your marketing? Why?

You are not expected to become a professional designer. Research and use affordable resources like DIY design site Canva and we builders like Wix, WordPress, Squarespace. Regarding websites, there are free and paid versions, but a paid version is required when you want to connect it to your own domain name. The point is to make this quick, painless, and easy, so that you don't need to reinvent the wheel. You may need different versions of visuals for different settings, square versus rectangular, or something optimized for a mobile phone. When in doubt, get affordable help from recommendations from colleagues.

Open a free Canva and Wix account, select a few of the templates with designs you want to use in your marketing and website.

Copywriting is the stealth ninja marketer. Great copy (the term for writing used in all aspects of commerce) is a joy to read. Sometimes you don't know why you keep reading, that's usually attributable to strong copywriting. Collect good newsletters and websites that you like. Below points show guidance for descriptions of products or services, writing your newsletter and website:

- Clarity first
- Write to one person
- Keep the tone personal
- Shorter, basic language
- Keep the main thing – the main thing

Imbue the "personality" of your brand in your language. That translates the "voice" of your writing. It may be fun but not silly, confident and cocky, expert but not bossy, weird but not inappropriate, or whatever you like. Voice encapsulates the way writing sounds and includes language, slang, and vocabulary choices as well as sentence structure. (Speak the copy aloud to help you hear that.) Voice is the personality, while the tone of your messages may be helpful and polite.

Remember to "do you"! Derek Sivers, musician, writer, and entrepreneur that founded CD Baby, wrote the best of all emails. It bucks the tide and is so fun, it's been shared all over the place. I remember receiving it after buying a CD from the company and forwarded it to everyone: https://sive.rs/cdbe. A tiny excerpt from that email:

> A team of 50 employees inspected your CD and polished it to make sure it was in the best possible condition before mailing. Our packing specialist from Japan lit a candle and a hush fell over the crowd as he put your CD into the finest gold-lined box that money can buy.
>
> We all had a wonderful celebration afterwards and the whole party marched down the street ....

Tools for writing:

- www.Wordhippo.com
- www.UrbanDictionary.com
- Emotion for writers: https://onestopforwriters.com/emotions
- Fun visual thesaurus: https://www.freethesaurus.com/Five+senses

Marketing with an authentic voice might include crafting a caricature who speaks to your audience or fans. Removing the completely personal dimension helps certain creatives maintain distance and perspective. Also, it lets you off the hook if you're someone who struggles with writing about yourself. Consider adding satire, personification of your offering, or hyperbole.

The magic of copywriting is both artistic and functional. Keywords and SEO are vital tools in online marketing. Keywords (the most often used words that relate to your business) and SEO (how you structure content in terms of sentences, headings, title tags, image labels, alt-tag keywords, and meta data online) all help you capture more leads online. The most important thing is to get in the mindset of your fans. What kind of questions would they type in if they are trying to find someone like you and what you sell? The more you understand how they think, the better you can shape your copy online to help them find you.

SEO and Web Discovery. Your audience interests drive SEO keywords, and how you are discovered online. (Keywords will be repurposed as your

#hashtags in social sharing.) You can do a keyword search to determine the competition of certain phrases through Moz (offers a free trial), Google AdWords Keyword Planner, KWPlanner, or Keyword Tool.

Grab your startup journal. What are the top 10 keywords that will help potential buyers find you and your offering? Write up a description of your MVP using those keywords, and copy that you believe will appeal to your customers.

The more defined, the better it is. Avoid overly generic terms that are highly competitive. The higher the competition is for a topic or term, the lower your chances are for ranking for that topic. So start big, but then drill down for specific topics like "colorful abstract oil painter in Denver, Colorado." Try adding your location or other information so that you have a more defined segment than just "painter" or "artist." SEO makes up much of what we see and interact with on the web.

It doesn't matter how great your artwork is or how beautiful your website is if it's not optimized for buyers to find it. Google crawls your site, and also your image tags. Instead of having an image on your site like IMG092382. tif, change image alt-tags to a relatable search "funny-affordable-custom-dog-portrait" or whatever it is that you want people to find.

Tip: Use dashes between your alt-tag keywords.

Demonstrate your web page value by sharing your content and linking. The Internet is in fact a popularity contest. Google favors content and pages that are valued (value to Google = clicks), and they will rank these pages higher as they assume that most people found these pages useful for their search. SEO can take a few months to build and develop as your links become more credible and authoritative.

It is definitely a marathon and not a sprint, but the payoff will also be long-lasting.

Email marketing is one of the most effective and cost-effective tools as well. Cultivate and build your list regularly and focus on using email as a tool to build relationships with your people. Write a newsletter about something significant – launching, your first service, new product, or something similar.

■ Decide who it is to and personalize it (Dear First Name:)
■ Keep it focused
■ Include a call to action
■ Make it attractive
■ Include two links

- Test before sending
- Make the email shareable to help grow your list
- Get into a sustainable cadence – maybe it's once per month, once per season, or weekly (don't spam)
- Provide value and amplify what you do

Open up a free newsletter service (like Mailchimp). Compose your first newsletter.

Websites are an important home base for your startup. A website is always open, 24/7, all over the world. Once you have it, people can find you and learn about what you do, effortlessly. Follow best user practices. That means design, functionality, and having a mobile site. You will need a contact form, information about you, and what you sell at the minimum. You can hire someone to do it for you and set it up, then you maintain it. DIY builders such as Wix, Squarespace WordPress, and GoDaddy offer attractive, functional templates. If you struggle with technology, utilize a service that sells all the components, domain, website, and hosting. Companies like GoDaddy offer a phone service, which is becoming more unusual. If you think you'll need that hands-on touch, search for a company with robust customer service.

A website is built up of three components.

1. The actual website is a construction of pages – what visitors see. Typical websites include a home page, contact form, call to action, services or products descriptions, store. You may include a blog, portfolio, and more. Start simply and then add more
2. A domain name – your online address on the web is how people find you, such as www.IamFairlyAwesome.com. If you're constructing a website separate from your online store, match the name as much as possible. You must pay for a URL yearly. It's possible to run a business entirely on social media, bypassing a website. However, if the site changes the rules, or something happens to it, you're out of luck. With a domain name, as a paying customer, you have more control
3. The hosting plan provides the real estate that your website rests upon. All of the companies mentioned sell that real estate, as well as Bluehost, SiteGround, and many others

A danger of websites and domains is that you want something that doesn't relate to what you do and then don't actually make it easier for people to find you. Some people buy a domain – then find out that related social handles are not available.

Search online, and select your domain, socials, and where you will build and maintain a website. Construct a basic site.

Schedule a reminder on your phone to check your site every month, take 5 minutes and make sure everything works and looks right. If the process of getting a website running seems like too much, hire a freelancer to do it for you.

Social Media. You don't need to be everywhere, just in the obvious places where your buyers spend time. Select one to two few platforms at first. Posting at a cadence and style that feels natural. If your potential people don't use those platforms, don't waste your time.

It will take a while to see the different content your fan, users, and buyers respond to, so don't stress. Play with it. Identify:

■ Two to three platforms where your people are
■ Best day/times to post
■ Vary your posts (not all can be sales)
■ Share relevant content of others

Have fun and don't overdo this – social media is a vortex. Follow thought-leaders in your field. Plan to automate and repurpose content. If you write a blog, use that in your newsletter and socials. If you write good social content, include that in your newsletter, and if you have one, your blog. A social media calendar is a simple way to plan and write posts ahead. A social media dashboard service helps you post in advance. Schedule time regularly to engage with fans/followers. Get familiar with the lingo, posting style, the platforms you use. Platforms include:

■ Snapchat	■ Facebook	■ Twitter	
■ LinkedIn	■ Amazon	■ TikTok	
■ Pinterest	■ Instagram	■ Tumblr	
■ Flickr	■ YouTube	■ Vimeo	
■ Soundcloud	■ BandCamp	■ CDBaby	
■ Deviant Art	■ Art Station	■ Reddit	■ Quora
■ Digg	■ Stumble Upon	■ Bored Panda	■ Good Reads
■ Clubhouse	■ HouseParty	■ Twitch	■ Discord
■ TikTok	■ IMdB		

The goal of social media is sales. Yes, I said it. Not all social media will generate sales. You build sales by building relationships. Remember that people want to buy from those that they like, sometimes admire, and feel some kinship with.

You can utilize social media to:

1. Discover and interact with your people
2. Help people sharing info, resources, and ideas
3. Build social capital.
   – in the goal of sales.

Listen to conversations, contribute what you can. Great posts can include sharing content from others, celebrating your community and individuals by reacting to their engagements, news, and content (Figure 4.6).

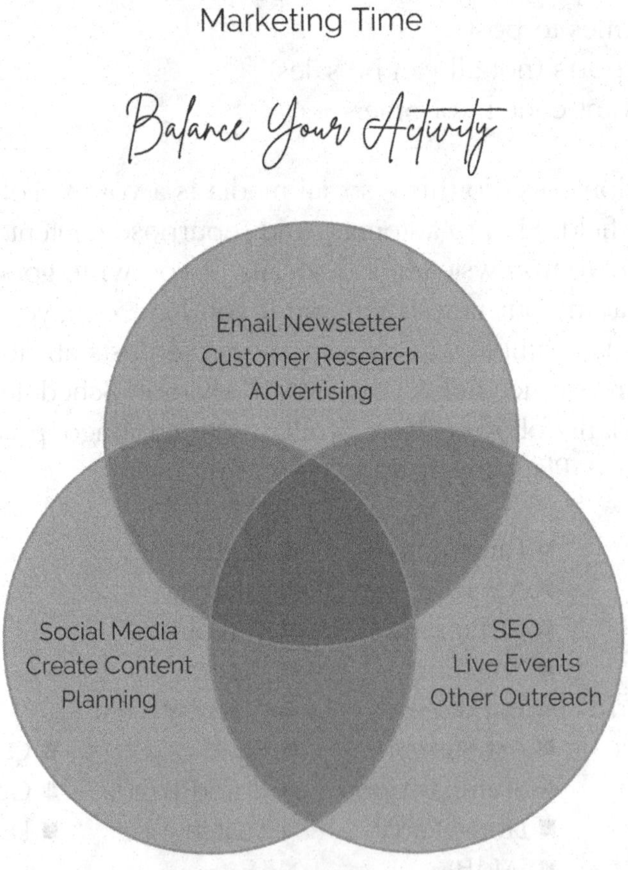

Marketing Time

Balance Your Activity

Email Newsletter
Customer Research
Advertising

Social Media
Create Content
Planning

SEO
Live Events
Other Outreach

Figure 4.6 Marketing Time by Paula Landry.

Make a plan, follow it. And, follow your intuition. If 15 minutes is spent engaging with one person, is that too long? Maybe not if it reassures them into purchasing. But why plan a tweet for 25 minutes? If you can't stand a platform, even if your buyers are there, you don't have to use it. Remember that at the end of the day you can control your website and email list (as long as you maintain and pay for them). You will never control social media. At any time, YouTube or Snapchat can kick you off, your handle can get hacked (a Twitter Troll ate mine). All the content that you built can vanish. Grow your website, your email list, and your store.

Social media sites share certain functions. If you understand these basic functions, you can more easily adapt.

Common tools:

- Username: What you call yourself
  Follow: Consider who and why
  Hashtag: (#) with words to discover with ideas or community

The Internet can be a dark place. Keep an attitude that reflects your values and shares positivity. Lead with transparency, authenticity, and generosity. If someone upsets you online, or you're unsure about posting something, skip it. Remember to spread your message by amplifying it by using # (hashtag) of keywords and @ (At – username) of the people and brands that may find value in your messages. Take inspiration from others and credit the great content of others. Mix it up in a way that's fun for you.

Types of social content:

- Opinions, current events, sharing ideas
- Letter from the Editor
- Photos, lists, videos
- How to's
- Games/polls/contests
- Deep dives
- Quick overview
- Rants, reviews, top 10s
- Holiday
- Throwbacks/nostalgia
- Tips/trips
- Secrets

- Branded/sponsored posts
- Fiction/on-fiction
- Vocab/lingo
- Opinion, comics, and critique
- Games, quizzes, contests, fundraisers
- Social causes and activism tools
- Profiles
- Advertisements

Promotional calendars offer creative freedom and a way to plan ahead. Some social media is best "in the moment" interactions with your audience, but most content should be planned ahead. It's efficient and helps you maintain your brand standard. Stick to the themes that compliment your company, and use a calendar to organize your content strategy. Figure 4.7 shows one such example.

Social Media Calendar

For Planning Ahead

Jan	Feb	Mar
Theme: Monthly Newsletter Social Media 3X Weekly Facebook, Twitter, Instagram Press Release	Theme: Monthly Newsletter Social Media 3X Weekly Facebook, Twitter, Instagram Event: Workshop	Theme: Monthly Newsletter Social Media 3X Weekly Facebook, Twitter, Instagram Contest
Apr	**May**	**Jun**
Theme: Monthly Newsletter Social Media 3X Weekly Facebook, Twitter, Instagram Press Release	Theme: Monthly Newsletter Social Media 3X Weekly Facebook, Twitter, Instagram Event:Charitable Fundraiser	Theme: Monthly Newsletter Social Media 3X Weekly Facebook, Twitter, Instagram Contest

Figure 4.7 Social Media Calendar by DeAngela Napier and Paula Landry.

You don't have to include a gazillion themes and post constantly. Many people use a newsletter or blog as the basis of content and build around that, copying parts of it for social media. Create a system and be consistent. Every so often, mix it up and see what changes.

Grab your startup journal and create a relaxed social media promotional calendar:

- What will you post?
- When will you post it? (day of week/times)
- Where will you post it?
- What type of content or themes?
- Which tools will you use?
- Have fun, have fun, have fun

Social media dashboard services save time, with a one-stop-shop to plan and disseminate content to several platforms. Some companies offer a free version with limited functionality (and show their branding). Paid versions offer more choices. Only use them if they make sense and are easy.

- Canva.com (www.canva.com)
- HootSuite (www.hootsuite.com)
- Sprout Social (www.sproutsocial.com)
- Socialbakers (www.socialbakers.com)

Initially, the job of any brand is to gain awareness with the most important target audience. Over time you'll want to broaden and diversify the audience, deepening the relationships. Become aware of the conversations going on in online communities by listening, so you're aware of current sentiment and topics. When you can, share your knowledge. There's no one-size-fits-all approach. Observe how others succeed, and experiment to find what works best for you.

Social proof is any confirmation from the public. This reassures buyers. Testimonials from clients, fans, and audience members are helpful. Another form of public praise that's highly regarded includes any mentions in the press. The "press" whether it's a blog, magazine, local paper, or other publication can appear to be a strong endorsement.

Public relations consist of a practice of deliberately managing the spread of information about your startup. One way to do that is to consistently

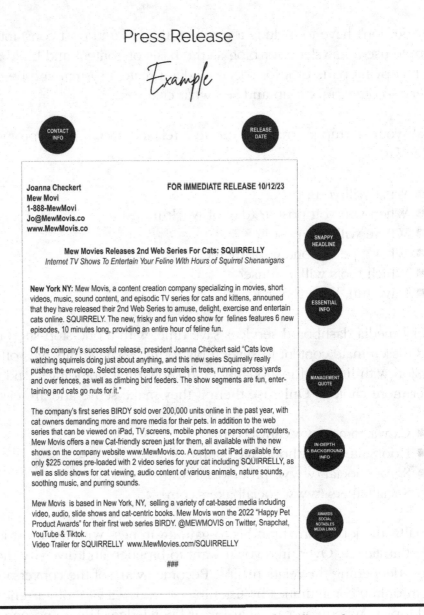

Figure 4.8 Press Release Format by DeAngela Napier and Paula Landry.

create press releases and disseminate them in blogs, local magazines, and newspapers. The press release format is designed to help journalists easily find relevant information for use in a story and follow-up (Figure 4.8):

There are a few rules about writing a press release to help attract attention:

■ Provide contact information
■ Post date of release
■ Make your headline short and interesting with verbs and clear language

- Make facts obvious: Who, What, Why, Where, and How
- Make the information as newsworthy as possible
- Offering a provocative quote from management
- Share background information, links, images, and media

As your company grows, you can build a targeted media list with 10–15 writers who cover your topic, industry, location, or field. As you create new offerings and become more confident, pitch send your press release to them in an email.

Marketing Budget

Knowing what to spend, and what you ultimately get from that expense is a way to market efficiently. The more you promote and examine your results – sales, likes, web traffic, gigs, commissions, etc. – the more you can refine your promotions. Some of the line items might include:

- Creative services or software
- Technical help if needed from consultants/freelancers
- Website, hosting, and domain
- Email newsletter, social media scheduling software, and design software
- Advertising (boosted posts, Google Ad campaigns)

You can always add or delete whatever makes sense for you.

For new businesses, marketing is a larger percent of the overall budget than for more established organizations. When you're just launching a product or service, there will be a period of experimentation to find audiences efficiently. You don't have to buy advertising right away. Once you're ready to try ads, allocate very modest amounts at first to see what works. Boosted posts on social platforms can be very affordable. Search ads can be very expensive, depending on the words you buy. If you try to buy search ads from Google, using common terms, like the word "FILM," it will be very expensive because many industries and companies use that word. The more targeted terminology you can use, and the more you define the results you're looking for, the more effective advertising campaigns will be.

A marketing budget for startups is usually calculated as a percentage of your projected (anticipated) sales for that year. It can be impossible to know this when you're just starting out. Once you have a handle on that information, and you anticipate selling $XXXX in your first year, you could plan to spend 25–30% of that amount on marketing. Marketing costs are generally higher for service companies than for companies selling products. As you generate revenue, you'll have more understanding of what to spend. An initial marketing budget may include help to design and build a website, and/or essential software or online service such as Canva in order to get going. The focus should be on profits, the money after expenses. If you have too many expenses, you'll never get profits. The goal is to balance your marketing budget so that you earn profits as quickly as possible.

Customer Acquisition Cost

Once you get a customer, remember that they are extremely valuable. For every $1 you spend to reach a current customer, it takes an average of $6 to reach a new customer. Nurture your buyer relationships, stay in touch, and reward them. Current customers can become your best marketers. Your cost to acquire a customer (customer acquisition cost) is a key metric that you will discover over time and sales.

Over time, as you grow sales and customers, you can project how much it will cost to acquire each one. You may plan that figure, but actual sales make it clear what those costs actually are (Figure 4.9).

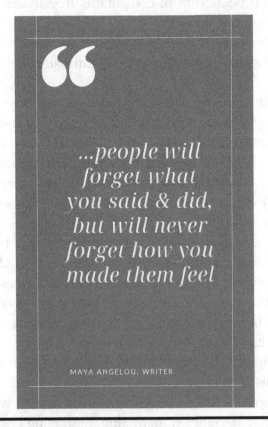

> ...people will forget what you said & did, but will never forget how you made them feel
>
> MAYA ANGELOU, WRITER

Figure 4.9   Quote by Maya Angelou.

To wrap up, the sharing of your offering with the world should be a two-way street. It consists of staying aware of what your customers think and want, while sharing the value that products and services can offer. As you proceed through the marketing process, have fun, and let your personality shine through in whatever you're doing.

Chapter 5

Generate and Launch

Generating is a process of movement. When your idea is in motion it will generate many things, primarily information: information related to the effectiveness of your tactics and additional information from sales, feedback, social media engagement, customer traffic, and inquiries. This will generate emotions, and you may need to manage them. Launching is putting your startup in public.

You may be keyed up due to the significant amount of time and work you've spent. A public launch may cause swings in your physical and mental energy. That's normal. Practice self-care; do whatever will help you, be it exercise, eating well, good sleep, meditation, baths, journaling and communicating with your support network.

Launch

Once you have set your startup in motion, you will generate results with the official launch. Woo hoo!

What is launching?

- Your offering is ready to be made public
- You have a product, service, or experience to sell
- OR/AND You have content to launch on the platform you are launching
- You have defined clearly how customers pay you
- That purchase process has been tested and works

DOI: 10.4324/9781003225140-5

■ You know how your offering is unique and how it will benefit your customers
■ You are sharing your offering with the public in various ways

This transition to launching is moving from beta, a private and contained group (often more forgiving) to the public (not always a kind audience). Look at it as a learning experience, rather than a make or break point.

Whatever happens, you can refine your MVP. Don't let analysis create paralysis. Most information is actionable, even if it can be uncomfortable. A lack of information is also actionable, indicating something isn't connecting (Figure 5.1).

It's not unheard of to feel nervous, or suddenly want to sabotage yourself. Or put off your launch. That's the fear (self-doubt, imposter syndrome) talking. It's perfectly normal but don't give into it. Move a launch date once if you absolutely have to, but hold yourself to keep that.

It's often said in the startup world that if you're not embarrassed by your MVP, you waited too long. Innovative companies like Pixar are protective of

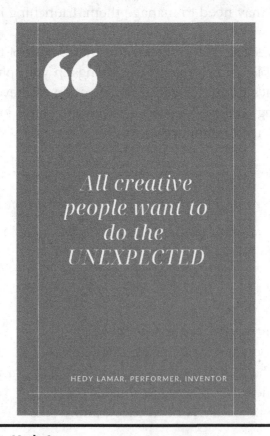

Figure 5.1 Quote by Hedy Lamar.

the director's "ugly babies" and encourage directors to create and share them internally, so they can be improved. It takes so many tries until a company can release a masterpiece, animated movies like *Toy Story* or *The Incredibles*. Forgive yourself any mistakes during this process, practice positive talk.

Visualize and Recall Your Skills. Activating your success mindset, recall an occasion that you launched a successful event, party, artwork, holiday, class project, group activity, anything. Channel that energy.

If you get overwhelmed, take a moment. Acknowledge your feelings, move your body to relieve tension. Feel like sabotaging yourself? Tell an accountability partner or friend. Let them talk you out of it. You'll learn as you go.

Timeline

As preparation, schedule your launch by creating a countdown. Take inventory of any takeaways from the beta process. Use some of that knowledge in a cost-effective and fast way. Prioritize carefully.

Include time for testing and refinement of the payment process, the customer experience, generating buzz, and marketing. Make a checklist of what needs to be refined immediately before launch, and other items that can wait. Address only the immediate items.

Countdown checklist:

- Adjust MVP if needed
- Test payment, functionality, and the technical process
- Legal considerations, (DRM) digital rights management
- What data are you going to collect and how
- Refine marketing copy, images, site, activities, and teaser info
- Get technical help if required
- Start buzz "it's coming soon!" marketing
- Address any creative issues (design, copy)
- Proofread every text item (ask a friend to help)
- Test the customer experience, go through the entire journey several times
- Share your plans with your beta testers and enlist their help
- Ask others to share your launch
- Invite press if that's part of your strategy (Figure 5.2)

Grab your startup journal and create your launch countdown timeline.

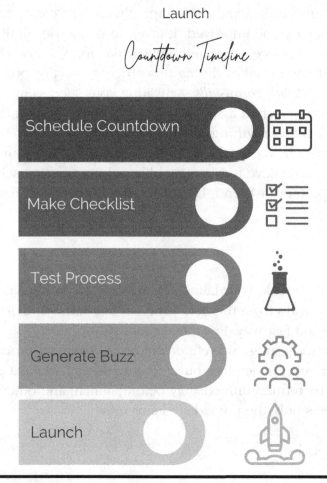

Launch

Countdown Timeline

Schedule Countdown

Make Checklist

Test Process

Generate Buzz

Launch

Figure 5.2 Countdown to Launch by Paula Landry.

If you've heard the same comments from beta testers multiple times, consider making that adjustment, maybe now or later. There's a balance in the MVP, it should be minimum in that you need what you sell to be minimal enough to get it to the public without waiting YEARS, but it must also be viable. It should deliver on what you're promising.

Think about protections that might be needed for your creations and can be put into place relatively easily. When creating digital media or artwork, entrepreneurs should consider protecting them using DRM (Digital Rights Management). DRM includes limits on copying, sharing, printing, and other attributes of the media. Think about this carefully. For instance, if I create a digital download and prohibit any printing, then that may be frustrating to a buyer. A difficulty of digital goods is they are easily shared, but as long as they can be identified that you are the creator, sharing may have the benefit of marketing. Be transparent with your customers. Programs like Adobe Creative Suite offer controls over what other people can do with your digital files.

When you move from your beta mode into a launch, the first thing you will be generating are results, information, feedback, financial, or otherwise. While it's easy to feel excitement and set expectations high, remember that this information will help you with your next steps. Nobody can tell you not to feel your feelings. Feel them. If the launch doesn't generate what you expected, but only a certain number of customers or sales (sign ups, hits, calls, email opens, likes, subscriptions, ticket purchases, referrals), acknowledge your feelings and process them. Then figure out what happened. Be patient, it may take time for customers to find you. If you receive no traffic online, look at your marketing. Is it connecting?

On Launch day, keep an eye on your store or site, to make sure it's working properly, keep marketing and sharing. Gauge customer responses or feedback. Ask partners for support in advance (encourage them to visit your site, spread the word, and purchase).

Mini Case Study. Musical indie vocalist, global touring artist, and songwriter Maya Azucena has won awards for her music and humanitarian outreach. Azucena garnered a Grammy Certificate for her vocal work with Stephen Marley on Best Reggae Album of the Year, "Mind Control." In a conversation with Maya, the turning point for her career came when she took the lead and looked at herself as an entrepreneur. The following is paraphrased from our conversation:

> As an entrepreneur, you are your own boss. This is a shift in mentality. Employees wait to be told what to do, go here at this time, do this by this date. You have to shift your mentality from you waiting around for someone to tell you to do things.
>
> You have to view yourself as an employer. Then say "I need to have these things completed, I need to show up on time for these things." If you treat your business like a hobby you'll have hobby results. Imagine if I open a store that's only open for 20 minutes, every three weeks. Is anyone going to shop at my store? Inconsistency is the killer. Consistency is the key to progress. Now imagine a store that's open 1 hour every single day, at the same time. It's not open as long as you might want but people can find and rely on. Now your store is in existence. This is the first thing – you have to be in existence to begin with. And then consistency, because other things can be built on something that's consistent.

You can find her at her website, https://mayaazucena.com/ on Spotify and @mayaazucena on Instagram.

Of the many takeaways from Maya's guidance, being consistent with your mindset and proactive work – will help your startup emerge and take shape. You need to be present before, during, and after your launch, so that people can come to find you, rely on you, and buy from you.

In addition to sales, you'll want to set up and track data. Set up the type of information that will enable you to understand your launch.

Set Up Data and Analytics

Here's the thing. You don't have to measure data and analytics. You can simply see if you garner sales, yes or no. Especially if you're feeling a bit swamped. However, it can be extremely valuable to measure your launch and understand the results. Then you understand what to tweak for an improvement.

At the end of the day, strive to understand:

- Who are your customers
- Where did they come from
- What actions did they take

If you have your own website, Google Analytics is a powerful analytical tool. By signing up for a free analytics account, you receive a block of code that you add to pages in your website. When a visitor to your website views a page, this code tracks information for Analytics. Whether you use the Google Analytics tool or dashboards from other websites, observe your web traffic, time spent on various pages, and where your traffic originated.

Whether you use digital tools like Google analytics, or data from your web host, website, and social media channels, or just tracking phone calls, or email inquiries, make sure that the tools are in place to capture that data so you can analyze it (Figure 5.3).

By observing these data over time, you can adjust your strategy for increased traffic, stickier pages where your visitors spend more time. Over time you may desire more information or more detailed information.

Create and log into a free Google Analytics account. Copy that code and include it in your online website or store. If your existing website or store has a data analytics dashboard, take a few moments and see what activities they measure.

Data

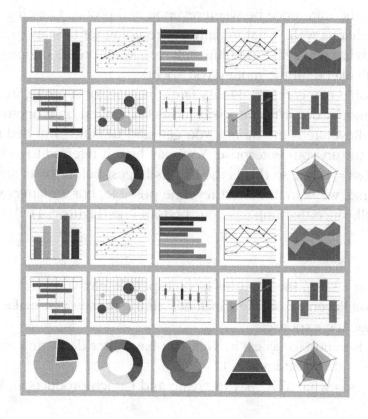

Various Inforamtion Can Be Used
To Analyze Your Startup

Figure 5.3 Data Dashboard. Image by Yvette from Pixabay, CC0.

Earning Revenue and Profitability

One of the first things you'll look at during your launch is revenue. During your launch, securing sales is not always the same thing as profits. The difference between the two is the expenses you have incurred. Creating revenue goals can serve as a strong incentive. If you are generating money, but you aren't profitable, you're spending more than you're making. That may indicate that you should fine-tune your business model. Take a look at whether there is a seasonality or cyclicality in the buying habits of your customers.

One way to examine the difference between revenue and profitability is by going back to the simple budget created earlier. Your budget and expenses probably included what was spent so far to get your venture launched. That number, the total amount you spent on your various startup expenses, is the difference between revenue and profits. Ongoing expenses will impact that as well. What initially you're going for is sales (people paying you for what you sell), and ultimately you want profits (money left over after you calculated all the money you spent).

What people pay is referred to as sales, income, or revenue, interchangeably. This amount doesn't reflect your costs (expenses) on a one-time basis, or ongoing. Revenue is the money you get paid BEFORE you deduct what it costs you to run your enterprise. You may hear it referred to as Gross Income (gross = large) so this is the $ at its largest before costs are taken out. Of course, we want the most revenue possible, but it matters what is spent as well, since that impacts your bottom line (Figure 5.4).

Terms

- Revenue = sales, income (this is what people pay you)
  - Gross Revenue (or sales) includes all the money you make prior to deducting expenses
  - Net Revenue (or sales) is what you have after deducting expenses (this is the "bottom line")
- Expenses = what YOU pay to create and launch products and services to sell
- Breakeven = when you've made as much as you've spent so far
- Profits = $ you made after you deduct what you spent on expenses. (Revenue − Expenses = Profits or Loss)
- Loss = $ when you've spent more than you've earned

If you sold services and products that generated $1,000 and spent $400 to do so, the $1,000 is revenue and $400 is expenses. Your profit would be the difference, $1,000 − $400 – you would have profited $600. Nicely done!

$1,000 Sales
−$400 Expenses
$600 Profit

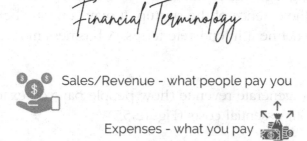

Essential

Financial Terminology

Sales/Revenue - what people pay you

Expenses - what you pay

PROFIT	BREAKEVEN	LOSS
Earned more than you spent	Earned the same as what you spent	Earned less than you spent

Figure 5.4 Essential Money Terminology by Paula Landry.

In order to create tangible profits, create revenue targets. Recall your SMART goals. Get specific, measurable, action-based, reasonable, and time bound. These revenue goals can work as incentives moving forward with your startup.

Grab your startup journal:

- Choose a specific # of your first product/service to sell
- Is it measurable and money-making
- What actions do you take to track this information
- Is it realistic and what resources do I need to do this
- In what time period do I want to do this and how will I track it

I will sell _____ # of my product/service by _____ date.

Business Model Review

In the startup language, the terminology of "business model" is used frequently. It is the essence of the startup. It may continue being refined, but you need to define it in concrete terms. A business model has two basic parts:

1. How do you generate revenue (how people pay you exactly)
2. What are your essential costs (Figure 5.5)

Guy Kawasaki, a brilliant entrepreneur and advisor to many successful companies, frames this as a straightforward concept. To paraphrase, "Who has your money in their pockets, and how will you get it into your pocket?" His focus on the business model is blunt. Aim for a very definable niche audience; keep your business model simple and easily understandable (10 words or less); copy someone else's business successful model (but innovate on the actual business concept itself).

In your startup journal, revisit your business model, state each part as concisely as possible.

As you go forward, the idea is that you learn to boost your revenue while reducing expenses without affecting quality. Understanding your business model and what makes you unique, and stating them succinctly (to yourself and others) will help you tremendously. The next step (and this may continue to crystallize over time) relates to how customers benefit from what

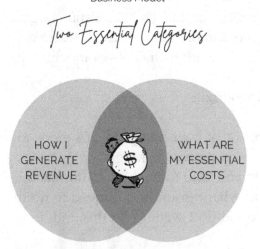

Figure 5.5 Business Model by DeAngela Napier and Paula Landry.

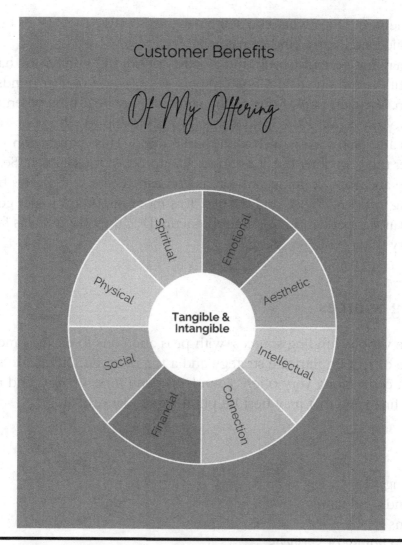

Figure 5.6   Offering by DeAngela Napier and Paula Landry.

you're selling. Your offering is the articulation of what you sell, with the specific benefits to customers.

In your startup journal, articulate your offering, those key benefits to your customers (Figure 5.6).

Cyclicality and Seasonality

Look ahead to your ultimate launch date, and you may or may not be overwhelmed by the results of your first week or two of sales, but it's important to look at the calendar on the wall. Many businesses have certain cycles or rhythms to them. People buy certain items more or less, depending on the time of the year. Does what you sell have a seasonality to it? Does buyer interest fluctuate in any kind of pattern?

This may not pertain to you, but at least consider it. Purchasing habits may be influenced due to the holidays, tax season, end-of-year mindsets, and so on. Vacation period during the summer may be a time when your people are tuned out. Do consider this in relationship to who your target market is and plan your launch with that in mind. This information you may learn over time, so don't use it as an excuse to delay your launch. Seasons will come and go. Get going as soon as you can. There will always be something to learn, adjust, and change. It is more important to get going than to wait for perfect timing. Entrepreneurs DO, they have a bias for action. Try things and get going.

Funding Sources

There are various funding sources, with pros and cons to each. Some take a long time or require intricate strategy and a ton of work. Others are sporadic and don't come along very often. Founders spend time, energy, and money securing financing that may best be put toward a launch.

Sources:

- Savings
- Friends and family
- Loans
- Trade equity or services
- Bootstrapping
- Incubator or accelerator
- Crowdfunding
- Grants

Savings and extra money are the fastest way to get going. Friends and family are a classic resource for funding. They often believe in your dream and are investing in you. If you go this route, put something on paper that both people sign. Be careful, as money has ruined many relationships.

Some banks specifically offer loans to small businesses, but it's hard unless you have collateral, good credit, and help with the loan application. The SBA (SBA.Gov) might help you with the application process. It can be difficult to qualify for a loan without any sales or sufficient collateral (assets that are valuable for the bank to take if you can't pay the loan back). If you find an alternative lender that seems to easily offer money for the loan, READ THE TERMS CAREFULLY, the interest rate may be high, or repayment terms may be difficult in some other fashion.

Some entrepreneurs trade equity (ownership in the startup) in exchange for services. Others create a barter arrangement between two parties, rather than a financial arrangement. You may perform tasks for one person, and they repay you with other help; it must be balanced.

Bootstrapping is the approach of self-funding with whatever resources you have, launching as frugally as possible.

- Rely on your skills and use what you have (sweat equity) and your own money
- Don't buy if you can rent something
- Don't rent if you can borrow something
- Trading skills and bartering it's fair

Incubators and accelerators for startup businesses can be found in major cities and in some colleges. Community, opportunity, and mentorship may be offered. There aren't any guarantees of funding through these organizations, just exposure to potential funders. Crowdfunding is very popular but is labor-intensive. Depending on the platform, how well you create your campaign and whether you can go viral, this may be an option. Most likely, you'll raise less than you need and it will take significant time and energy. Grants are slow and unpredictable.

The biggest takeaway is don't wait. Don't use a lack of funds as an excuse to procrastinate.

Unless you are creating this venture at work for your employer, YOU are your major investor. Creating a business inside a company (intrapreneurship) can be fulfilling. You'll receive support and funding. This increases your value in an organization, but you won't own the end results. Also, you won't be completely independent during the process.

Whatever way you fund your startup, from self-funding to the other ideas listed here, they have various positive and negative attributes.

Investment. The saying goes that she or he who makes the gold makes the rules. It's very hard to take money from another person without them wanting you to take their advice as well. The best money is quiet money that will trust you to get this going, yet be receptive to asking opinions and reflections. This will come from a person who believes in you and wants you to succeed. By its very nature, the person who invests in your creative business has a stake in the game. They can get in one of a few ways. There are two types of investment, debt and equity.

Debt funding is a loan, with a specific amount, a date when it needs to be paid back by, and specified interest. Interest is an additional amount on top of the loan – essentially a fee you pay to the lender for letting them use your money.

Example: You borrow $1,200 from your favorite aunt. (This would be debt funding.) You both agree that you will pay her back, plus 5% annual interest, over the next year, so that the entire loan will be paid back by 1 year from now.

 5% of 1,200 is 60.
 As a calculation: $0.05 \times 1,200 = 60$
 You will need to pay her 1,260 by the end of the year.

Once you have completely paid her back, she may consider loaning you a bigger sum. This kind of social contract makes some people feel more committed to what they're doing and prouder when they succeed. No matter what deal you strike with a person, write it down and both of you should sign it.

Equity investors exchange money for ownership. Your aunt may give you $1,200 for a percent of ownership in your business. This is more complex because you're assigning a value to your business before you have a clear picture of the value. Remember to retain the majority of ownership or you will cease to control the venture. Investors profit when the company profits.

They can sell their shares in the business if she can find a buyer. But this is not a loan, so that money may never be repaid. Any equity investor needs to understand this, and it's critical so you don't harm the relationship, which is much more valuable than money.

Crowdfunding. Crowdfunding is one way to raise money online. There are several platforms where you run a campaign for something specific, people donate, and you provide them with an inexpensive token gift (perks, or some similar term) in return to say thank you. These token thank you's can be digital and experiential in nature, they do not have to be physical or cost you money. In fact, please don't use anything that must be mailed or take time. Make it digital, easy, and cheap (yet memorable) if you go this route.

The pros of crowdfunding are that you may exceed your goal and get extra funds, notoriety, and fans who didn't know you in the first place. If you do it right, this can be effective marketing. At the outset, my advice is to use the money you have, however modest, to get going and not wait to raise money. However, crowdfunding can be a marketing tool to build an audience, gaining new exposure with what you're up to. If you use it in that way to build your email list, find new audiences, it may be worth it. Avoid an "all or nothing" structure, where you won't get anything unless you reach a certain number. Choose an amount to raise that you know you can reach, get friends, family, and colleagues to commit to getting you there. If you do this, there's a chance the platform will recognize your momentum and push your campaign to a front page where it will be exposed to strangers who can get you to a much bigger number. Payment gateways and the platform will deduct fees from whatever you raise.

The cons of crowdfunding are that it is time consuming, is energy consuming, and may detract from the work on your venture which requires a certain laser focus. It takes research, planning, and time to nail one of these. Some are specific to a particular art form, make sure to do your homework. Kickstarter, Indiegogo, Seed&Spark, and Patreon are some of the established sites.

There are a few crowdfunding-like sites that allow equity investors to invest and take an ownership interest in your company as well. The fees are generally higher for the company receiving the funding. Fundable and WeFunder are two of these types of platforms. While they look and feel like crowdfunding because the platforms are similar, these are legal investments (governed by the SEC) and are more serious. It's more like equity funding from a crowd of strangers (who are notified of all the relevant risks). Your commitment to these funders is way more serious than sending a perk to someone for a typical crowdfunding campaign. Take time to carefully read and understand the rules, should you go this route.

Take a look at the various features and social networking tools the crowdfunding site offers. The most effective crowdfunding websites have access to help like chats or easy to search information, guidelines, and easy-to-use tools to share your campaign online in several places.

Fundraising Events. There are a number of innovative types of fundraising you can do for your venture, all of which will take time and energy. If it will serve your purpose of marketing, or press in addition to raising money, it may be worth it. That is ultimately for you to decide. Fundraisers can consist of a contest, auction, raffle, or an event such as a showing, launch party, or performance; the sky is the limit. If you have someone to help and great collaborators to pull something like this off, it might be worth it. Remember to keep costs as low as possible and design an event which suits your products and services. Creating a Caribbean food cookbook for sale? A fun event might be a tasting event with food and music to match or something else that is built around Caribbean culture.

Pros of fundraising include that you have an excuse to tell people what you're doing, your goals, how you're doing it, and let them join in on the fun. Through a fundraising event you can spread the word, possibly find beta testers and seek feedback.

Cons of fundraising are the time-suck, energy expenditure, and may backfire once you are selling your service or product if people feel like they already contributed, they may now want to pay you again. This depends largely on your network, relationships, and various other factors.

Grants. Grants provide funding from a foundation, non-profit, government body, family foundation, or other organization created specifically to give money away for certain causes. You are probably aware of many of them, the biggest, like The Ford Foundation, advertise what they do all around the world, and can make a substantial impact within a variety of donations in specific areas like health, education, and so forth. Most grants are awarded to non-profit organizations rather than individuals, however, there are grants for individuals.

The pros of grants are that they seem like free money with few strings attached other than documentation following up on what you did with the funds.

The cons of grants are that take an enormous of energy to research or even find, the schedules will not pertain to when you need the money, they take a significant amount of time to write with (must be written in a very specific way) little to no expectation of being awarded to you. This is a very slow process in general. Unless you are connected to a specific person at the grant-making organization who will help champion what you are doing, or you have a grant writer to do this work for you, it can be extremely time consuming.

Sponsorships. Sponsorships from one or more companies are a possibility if you can identify a natural synergy with an organization, and you have a relationship there. No matter what deal you strike with a company, write it down and both of you should sign it. Even better, ask a lawyer to look it over. The terms should be crystal clear, perhaps you are putting their logo on some of your work, social media, or website – clarify how many times per month that would be, and for how long a period of time.

Pros around sponsorship include exposure of your work to a wider audience and new opportunities.

Cons are the expense of your money and time, it's not easy to secure sponsorships. If something bad happens at the company, it may reflect on you. You generally will have less leverage than the company. The balance of benefits to each party may be uneven. However, if the benefits outweigh the securing, maintaining and delivering on promises you make to the sponsor, it may be worth it.

Why You Should Skip It

Initially, I encourage you to bypass these and come back to them once your MVP is out there. If that's not an option, crowdfunding would be my first suggestion. Every funding method is always more involved than one plans for, and the outcomes are uncertain. You could hire someone to help you, although that's another diversion of your energy that could go into your startup. There are websites of angel investors and other possibilities such as microbusiness investors. These are typically equity deals, an exchange of money for ownership. It's difficult to secure equity investment without some traction (sales) in the marketplace.

By committing your own funds, you are accountable only to yourself. You can focus on what you want. Others (potential customers) may provide feedback, but it won't be filtered through the lens of other people this needs to be your vision. If you invest your own money, you'll be beholden only to you. If you lose it, you'll work smarter and understand what happened and how to fix it. Seeking funding after you can share results makes more sense. People love momentum, you can use that.

Multiple Streams of Income

Once you launch, your MVP is in the world, congratulations!! That is amazing! You are fantastic! Take a moment and celebrate your efforts.

No matter how imperfect or nascent it may be, you did something monumental. And buoyed (hopefully) by this experience you know you can do it so you'll want to do it again, sooner than later, by adding a new product or service. It may be just like your Minimum Viable Product with a twist, a version of your MVP, or something different. The idea is to sell more things, generate $, and feedback, applying what you learn. That will help you earn recurring revenue and create multiple revenue streams.

No matter the amount, once your startup launches a product or service, it's time to consider the next. Creating and launching one product to monetize (sell) means you can do another. The idea is to generate several sources of income. If it's possible, consider launching a product, service, or experience that could be bought or paid for at regular intervals to generate recurring revenue, like a subscription. The advantage is that you build something once but sell multiple times, then you're creating a somewhat passive income stream (Figure 5.7).

Passive Income. The concept of passive income is that once you create a product or service, and put it up for sale, you're done. Unfortunately, that's not entirely realistic. Promotion and customer relations are ongoing. When

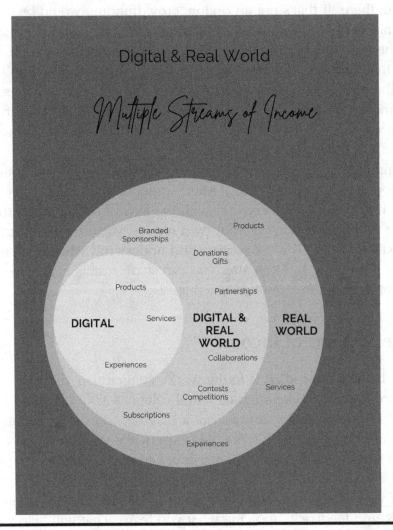

Figure 5.7 Multiple Revenue Stream Example by DeAngela Napier and Paula Landry.

you are selling a service, that's not passive at all. Once you sell the service, you must schedule and perform that service. It's similar to experiences. The only passive part is how much you can automate the process.

An example of passive income is a video class that you write, design, videotape, create the materials, and upload to a platform like Skillshare.com or Teachable.com. You should promote the course as much as possible, but to some extent it's a passive income source as people search for this class topic on that platform. As you add more products and services to complement the first, one may bring more revenue than others. It's one of the reasons we learn to launch quickly. Then you might make more like that. There's no way to be completely certain what hit. With every new offering, there's an opportunity to keep a conversation going with your customers.

What is something that seems like it would provide relatively passive income if you sold it? What are the next two to three experiences, products, or services you would like to sell?

Recurring Revenue

Recurring revenue is the dream for business, hoping that a buyer will pay repeatedly for something. As you go forward in your entrepreneurial journey, designing something to sell that can generate recurring revenue (which you don't have to keep engaging and selling to a customer since they're signed up for auto payment on something) should be considered as a goal if it fits with what you can sell.

Build Once, Sell Many Times

We love subscriptions. And at some point people may burn out on them, but for the moment it seems they are here to stay. Even non-traditional items can have a subscription idea to them. It's about your attitude toward sales and making things as easy as possible for your customer. By committing to buying something a few times per year, ahead of time, that takes no extra work on their part, with auto-billing, you can add a layer of convenience to your startup. Consider applying that kind of thinking and see if something jumps out at you.

Is there something you could sell in a subscription model?

To build recurring revenue into your business model, consider the types of features we see for this online. This type of "Automatic Opt In," means that the default purchase for a buyer selects buying again, automatically.

This is to save the person time and bother and benefits the seller. Always be transparent.

In the perfect world you want to build several streams of recurring revenue that will wax and wane naturally over time as you concentrate on new offerings. Feedback is key, so remember to ask your current customers what they need, want, and hope to have? Keep in touch with them via surveys and email (don't spam) and let them help you select the next product or service you sell. What do they most wish for that nobody else is helping them with? How do they want to feel and how can you make that happen? Ask these and other questions to get to know your people and tribe as well as you can and watch your business grow (Figure 5.8).

Generating your launch is a giant step forward. No matter how it is received in the world, the fact that you do it is a launch of its own. You have proved to the world, and yourself, that you can tackle something challenging. Continuing to refine, manage, and analyze your startup will help you to refine and improve your strategy and plan new offerings.

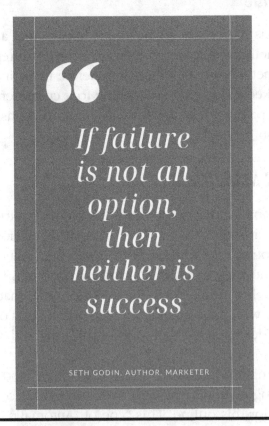

If failure is not an option, then neither is success

SETH GODIN, AUTHOR, MARKETER

Figure 5.8   Quote by Seth Godin.

Chapter 6

Manage and Analyze

Once you've gotten started with your launch, you need a rhythm for running your startup. That day-to-day process includes managing the overall workflow. A workflow consists of the various items you need to do including tracking and analyzing relevant information, prioritizing tasks, then identifying next steps. Scheduling the managing and analyzing of your venture depends on the cadence of your sales and your lifestyle. When one person is running a startup, management and administration are fused together.

For small businesses that many creatives run, managing may include everything from scheduling a wide variety of ongoing tasks and doing them.

What is managing?

- Figuring out what to do and when to do it
- Maximizing efforts toward profits
- Identifying new opportunities
- Prioritizing the creation of new offerings
- Performing management tasks to save time and money
- Perfecting your operations workflow and marketing process

Management tasks include banking, deciding which new offerings to focus on, research, marketing and engaging with customers, and automating whatever you can. At the end of the day, the point is to maximize profitability. By overseeing and tweaking HOW things are done, WHICH things are done and WHEN, you eliminate layers of effort that won't make you money. It's good to understand WHY efforts are made. If you're not

DOI: 10.4324/9781003225140-6

sure, stop doing something entirely. See what happens. Early on it's usually one person doing everything. That works for a while. As soon as possible, delegate or outsource what you can.

Within the first 3 months of operating, consider tax and legal details such as saving your receipts and protecting your intellectual property. Nobody expects you to become a lawyer or an accountant, but you should hire someone once you need them. Management includes analyzing revenue and marketing results, keeping basic IT and tech working so that "buy" and "pay" and "deliver" or "download" functions, and auto-responders work.

Something that can be helpful is to create Standard Operating Procedures (SOPs) so you don't have to learn everything all over again each time you do it. That could be a simple checklist or cheat sheet in your startup journal with steps for repetitive tasks, user names and passwords, and frequently visited sites or phone numbers. Figure it out once, and create a list of actions to make processes easier and faster.

Something that sets off a standard operating procedure is a trigger; an action (you receive an email from a potential customer) what do you do?

■ Create a list of steps – which may include opening your email account, answering the note within a half-hour, then following up the next day.
■ Add a checklist to guarantee you don't overlook a particular step (spell check or proofreading, for instance).
■ Also, establishing replicable procedures helps you delegate that activity to another person when you are in a position to do so (Figure 6.1).

In your startup journal, make a list of important items you'll need SOPs for regularly.

Analyzing your startup consists of collecting data, studying it to understand what it means, and acting it on that information when necessary.

Example: Your demographic information indicates that your target market includes both men and women. However, only women actually bought. Can the data reveal something about your offering or your approach in marketing. Analyze your data starting with questions.

1. Should I create a different male-oriented item that may appeal to men more?
2. Is the right approach to market items differently to men and women, so men will discover them?
3. Should I tailor all my efforts toward women customers for now?

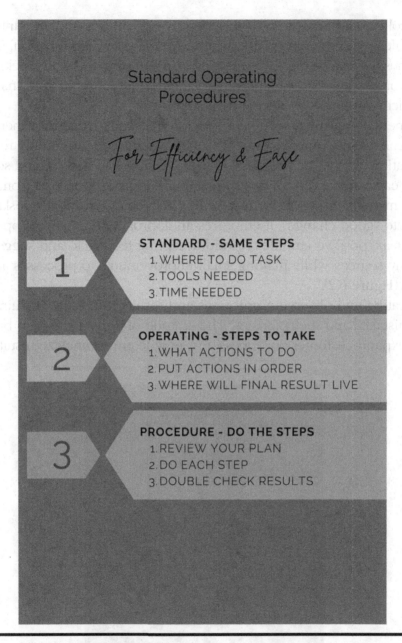

Figure 6.1 Standard Operating Procedures by DeAngela Napier and Paula Landry.

Analyzing your business includes:

- Deciding which data to collect and observe
- Setting up easy ways to gather relevant data
- Studying the data at regular intervals
- Learning from the data to make refinements
- Incorporating what you've learned

Data to collect and analyze may include buying patterns and amounts of final sales, who my buyers are, web traffic, seasonal information, and effectiveness of marketing. By collecting and studying the data weekly, monthly, or at some other regular interval, you may observe patterns over time, which will help you decide next steps.

Openness to learning, and incorporating that knowledge incrementally, has become an instrumental part of the startup model. Commonly referred to as iteration, this is the progression from version 1 to 2, to 3, and so forth.

The idea was adapted to startup practices, originating in part from the Japanese manufacturing sector inspired by Kaizen, a term that translates loosely into "good change." It embraces an approach to creativity, openness to new ideas, positive attitudes toward accepting feedback, and suggestions from many sources while making small improvements to processes and products (Figure 6.2).

By creating and observing processes and results mindfully, the aim is to reduce mistakes and inefficiencies. The attitude of kaizen can help build morale, expand customer awareness, test new features, analyze results, and

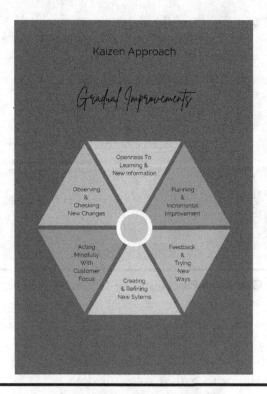

Figure 6.2   Kaizen by DeAngela Napier and Paula Landry.

build improvements into your startup gradually. Managing and analyzing your startup are interconnected, yet separate activities. Initially, certain tasks may take more time as you set up a repeatable process in order to become efficient.

A possible startup schedule if you are working 4 days a week on your venture might be to spread some of the duties over a portion of your overall startup time. Depending on a variety of factors, you may put all your time into this or fit this into some of your free time. The schedule should work for you.

- Day 1: creation
- Day 2: creation, marketing, and manage
- Day 3: creation, marketing, and manage/analyze
- Day 4: creation and marketing

Do one thing at a time, you'll figure out the best way as you do it. Remember when you first get started, time needs to pass to generate sufficient results to be able to analyze, so don't jump the gun. Look at results regularly, but don't assume you need to adjust anything your strategy immediately.

Visualize and Recall Your Skills. Remember to bring your unique talents and abilities into this process. Recall something you've done when you were successfully managing and analyzing a task. Whether you managed something for yourself or others, from a craft project to an event, occasion, or process, bring that confidence into this process. When you have analyzed anything satisfactorily in the past, for yourself or others, or made conclusions from the information you received, recall that sense of accomplishment. Visualize your success from then and channel that energy and positivity into this endeavor.

Administer Your Venture

Administering your startup includes the activities that will support your creative endeavor of designing and creating new offerings. The management and analysis of the performance of your products and services is part of that. Also, you'll want to make sure that your offerings are protected, as well as you personally. So that means putting a few things into place once you are ready to and understand the implications around these ideas. You'll want to know that your banking and taxes are as straightforward and simple as possible, that you can find information when you need it. This requires creating a few processes, and efficient organization of resources (time, money, energy, communication) to help the pursuit of your goals.

The amount of time to spend on the administrative duties of your startup depends on its overall complexity. Initially, there is a learning curve the first time you do something. Administering includes tasks that you will do several times, so the goal is to create a repeatable process that you understand. This relates to banking, taxes and money management, communicating with customers or vendors, various marketing, essential IT functions, as well as hiring help when you need it, and even essential legal duties, whether that is using a new contract or protecting your intellectual property.

Administrative duties should be scheduled into manager time, in shorter periods compared to creative tasks. At first, plan to attend to administrative work either once per week or every other week. As you proceed, it may be a good idea to adjust the schedule. These tasks would include:

- Planning and maintaining timelines and schedules
- Calendar management
- Communication with clients and partners – phone, email
- Filing, organize documents and paperwork
- Test website, create backups (make sure password, security works)
- Organizing and managing customer information
- Gather and track receipts, accounting, bookkeeping-related tasks
- Update legal, tax, financial info, and reports, if necessary
- Analyzing marketing information
- Training, if needed
- Create and maintain systems
- Recruitment, procuring vendors, or resumes if you need help

Schedule managing into your schedule on a regular basis.

Legal Concepts and Contracts

This is not a legal book. It doesn't substitute for working with a lawyer or legal advice. Creative people selling their goods, products, services, and experiences will encounter certain topics multiple times, so it is a good idea to study and understand how they relate to you. Especially when reading a contract, ask for help if you need it, make sure you understand it and ask questions.

Writing, music, design, performing, fashion, photography, performing arts, entertainers, creators all work in and around intellectual property, but each discipline has properties that are unique.

Three of the most commonly needed legal concepts by artists are understanding the nature of Intellectual Property, including what a work-for-hire is, knowing how to read and understand confidentiality agreements or NDA (non-disclosure agreement) as well as Independent Contractor agreements which sometimes have confidentiality language in them, and understanding when and why you may need a release.

Basic concepts around Intellectual Property

- Intellectual Property ("IP") is anything original that you create and is protected by U.S. law
- IP laws protect inventions (Patents), artistic works (Copyrights)
- Trademarks and Servicemarks exist to distinguish one company from another

Mini Case Study. Toni D'Antonio is the founder and CEO of Shake the Tree Productions, a company that creates and produces original creative content including TV, film, music, and more. She is also an award-winning actress and producer, as well as a voice-over artist. When she was first starting out in business, she kept in mind words from her mother, a brilliant woman, who reminded Toni to make sure she was always the smartest person in the room. So she studied contract law for several years. And by the time it came time to negotiate her first distribution deal for her movie, she knew the contracts inside and out. She still works with a lawyer but saves time and money because she's made it her business to understand the legal aspects of her work. She taught herself contract jargon, how to negotiate, create deal memos, file SAG paperwork, do workmen's comp paperwork, find what Errors & Omission insurance is and why it's needed, all of which gave her an enormous advantage. She is able to hang with the big boys and understand every aspect of her projects. In her mind, this is important, not just in the film business, but in any business. By understanding the legal aspects of your field, you don't miss a step, nobody can put anything over on you. To learn more about Toni and her creative content, visit http://www.shakethetreeproductions.com/

Regarding legal concepts, it's a good idea to:

- Research and find lawyers who understand and work with creatives
- Build a relationship with a lawyer with experience in intellectual property
- Understand the common agreements you'll need
- Create legal agreements you'll need multiple times

One topic that many entrepreneurs wrestle with is the proper timing to form a corporate entity. The timing of business structure, if any, and selection of what type of entity, entails several factors and has lasting effects.

Different Corporate Forms

Forming a company is a legal decision and you do not have to rush into it right away, for the simple reason that it has tax implications. Money spent and made initially will be as a sole proprietor, so it all relates to you (Table 6.1).

Discuss the pros and cons with a financial professional or tax adviser when you're ready to take that step. If you don't know one, locate one who is friendly to small businesses (SBA.gov) to make sure you understand. A lower-cost upfront may seem attractive, however, you may have to pay more down the line if you don't understand all of the details. Every state spells out details around the rules governing forming a business: https://www.usa.gov/state-business.

The Small Business Administration (SBA.GOV) describes key differences between entities.

Sole Proprietorship. You're automatically considered to be a sole proprietorship if you do business activities but don't register as any other kind of business. Your business and personal assets and liabilities are not separated. You can be held personally liable for the debts and obligations of the business. Sole proprietors can get a trade name, a DBA (doing business as) which you may need to have registered with your state or county, to do business using a name other than your own. It can be harder to raise money from others (excluding family and friends) because you can't sell stock, and banks are hesitant to lend to sole proprietorships.

Limited Liability Company (LLC) is the most common form for startups, once you're ready to take that step. An LLC has the advantage of the benefits of both the corporation and partnership business structures. It can

Table 6.1 Corporate Forms

Business structure	Ownership	Liability	Taxes
Sole proprietorship	One person	Unlimited personal liability	Personal tax only
Partnerships	Two or more people – be sure to understand the liability for the general partner	Unlimited personal liability unless structured as a limited partnership	Self-employment tax (except for limited partners) Personal tax
Limited liability company (LLC)	One or more people – be sure to understand the difference	Owners are not personally liable	Self-employment tax Personal tax or corporate tax
Corporation – C corp	One or more people	Owners are not personally liable	Corporate tax Double taxation for the owners
Corporation – S corp	One or more people, but no more than 100, and all must be U.S. citizens	Owners are not personally liable	Personal tax Discuss with Advisor versus LLC
Corporation – nonprofit	One or more people	Owners are not personally liable	Tax exempt, but income must be used for mission. Best used for cause-based efforts – social, artistic, educational, and health-related organizations

be formed with one person or multiple people. LLCs can protect you from personal liability and protect personal assets, like your vehicle, house, and so on (in most cases, not all). Profits and losses can get passed through to your personal income without facing corporate taxes. Every state is different, it's important to understand how the state that you form the LLC in will impact you.

Partnership. Partnerships are the simplest structure for two or more people to own a business together. There are two common kinds of partnerships: limited partnerships (LP) and limited liability partnerships (LLP). The term liability means taking legal responsibility.

Limited Partnerships have one general partner with unlimited liability, and all other partners have limited liability. The partners with limited liability also tend to have limited control over the company. Profits are passed through to personal tax returns.

Limited Liability Partnerships are similar to limited partnerships, but give limited liability to every owner. An LLP protects each partner from debts against the partnership; they won't be responsible for the actions of other partners.

Corporation – C Corp is a legal entity that's separate from its owners. This is the entity of some of the most prominent and largest businesses. This is the entity one forms when they intend to go public (launch an IPO). Corporations can make a profit, be taxed, and can be held legally liable. Corporations offer the strongest protection to their owners from personal liability, but the cost to form a corporation is higher than other structures, requiring more extensive record-keeping, operational processes, and reporting.

S Corp is a special type of corporation that's designed to avoid the double taxation drawback of regular C corps. S corps allow for profits, and some losses, to be passed through directly to owners' personal income without ever being subject to corporate tax rates. There are strict filing and operational processes.

Non-Profit Corporations are organized to do charity, education, religious, literary, or scientific work. Because their work benefits the public, non-profits can receive tax-exempt status, meaning that they don't pay state or federal income taxes on any profits. Non-profits must file with the IRS to get tax exemption, and this can be a lengthy process. They must follow organizational rules very similar to a regular C corp, and special rules about what they do with any profits.

When in doubt about forming your business entity, wait. Operate as yourself, a sole proprietor. This decision has a lasting impact, so discuss it with a lawyer or accountant, or be sure you understand how it will affect you.

The law exists to protect consumers, business owners, and relationships. No matter whether you have a lawyer or not, certain arrangements require some simple agreement. If you're working with another party, hiring them, or partnering, or accepting their funding, write down the arrangement. Maybe you won't need it, but it could prove valuable in the event any confusion or disagreement arises.

Legal Agreements. Three of the most commonly needed legal documents performers, artists, entertainers, and creatives use include confidentiality or non-disclosure agreement (NDA), some type of release, and an independent contractor agreement. Following are examples of each contract with a brief explanation.

People are asked to sign non-disclosure and confidentiality agreements in order to keep information private for a period of time, or in perpetuity (forever).

There is a one-way agreement, where one person, usually the signing party, agrees to keep the other's information confidential. Or the agreement could be mutual, a two-way NDA agreement, where both parties agree to keep each other's information confidential. Figure 6.3 shows a one-way

Sample Confidentiality Agreement

I, _____,_____,
acknowledge that the information provided by:

_____,_____,
included in the following document(s): is confidential in nature.

I agree not to share or disclose this information without the express written permission of:
_____,_____
for a duration of ____ years.

Upon request, this document will be returned immediately to:

Print Name:
Address:
Email
Phone:

My Signature _____
Date Signed _____

Figure 6.3   Confidentiality Agreement by Paula Landry.

agreement, where the person signing is agreeing to keep one person's/company's information private.

A video or photo release is a document that a model or person appearing in photos or videos agrees that the company or person shooting the images will own the resulting images and can do whatever they want (Figure 6.4).

The independent contractor agreement spells out a work relationship. It typically includes payment, description of work and deliverables (what is to

Sample Video / Photo Release

I _____,_____, being of legal age, hereby consent and authorize _____, (person's name, or company name), successors, legal representatives and assigns to use and reproduce a photograph(s) taken by _____ (videographer / photographer name) on _____ (date) and to reproduce my name (or any fictional name) in all forms and media now known and unknown, for any and all purposes including publication and advertising of every description, in perpetuity (forever) throughout the known and unknown universe. I will make no claim of any kind. No representations have been made to me. I hereby warrant that I am of legal age and have every right to contract in my own name; that I have read the above authorization and release prior to its execution, and that I am fully familiar with its contents.

Agreed:
Print Name:
Address:
Email / Phone:
Signature _____
Date _____

Figure 6.4   Video/Photo Release Template by Paula Landry.

be completed), a timeline, and the work-for-hire language. Work for hire is a statement that the independent contractor will not own anything created under this contract. No matter what the contribution of the independent contractor – the hiring party (whoever pays) will own the preliminary and final results. That means the hiring party will own all intellectual property rights, whether copyright or otherwise (Figure 6.5).

There are many other legal documents that you may need from an invoice, to a lease, to collaboration agreements. There are "Volunteer Lawyer

Sample Independent Contractor Agreement

Date_____

Dear _____: (person being hired)
The following outlines our agreement and summarize the terms of the arrangement that we have discussed. You have been retained by _____ (hiring person & or company name) as an independent   contractor   for   the   project   of _____. You will be responsible for successfully completing the above-described project according to specifications and within the policy guidelines outlined:
The project is to be completed by _____ (date)
at a cost not to exceed $_____ with payments as follows:
$_____ upon mutual execution of this agreement
$_____ upon _____ (date of approved delivery)
$_____ upon _____ (date of approved completion)

You will invoice us for your services rendered at the end of each month. We will not deduct or withhold any taxes, FICA, or other deductions that we are legally required to make from the pay of regular employees. As an independent contractor, you will not be entitled to any fringe benefits, such as unemployment insurance, medical insurance, pension plans, or other such benefits that would be offered to regular employees. During this project, you may be in contact with or directly working with proprietary information that is important to our company and its competitive position. All information must be treated with strict confidence and may not be used at any time or in any manner in work you may do with others in our industry. If you agree to the above terms, please sign and return one copy of this letter for our records. You may retain the other copy for your files.

Agreed:
Independent Contractor Signature _____
Independent Contractor Printed Name _____
Date Signed _____

Hiring Person Signature _____
Hiring Party Printed Name _____
Date Signed _____

Figure 6.5   Independent Contractor Agreement Template by Paula Landry.

for the Arts" organizations in most states and many big cities if you have questions or need a consultation. However, many law firms offer some pro bono work to people who really need and deserve it, so don't be shy about asking a firm if they have this program. Online legal services such as LegalShield.com, Nolo.com, and RocketLawyer.com are DIY alternatives and some of them include lawyer consultation components. While these are worth considering, cultivating a relationship with a trusted and knowledge-able lawyer versed in your field is a worthy, longer-term goal.

Protecting Your Intellectual Property

It is possible to generate income from intellectual property without protect-ing it. People do it all the time. However, it is important to understand what your intellectual property is, how it can be used (exploited) by you, and oth-ers, for profit. Protecting your IP creates more value. Whether you're selling something that is a copyright product or an invention that should be pro-tected by patent, you should protect it as soon as it's economically feasible. Copyright protection – which applies to intangible, artistic creations – is very affordable, while patent protection – which is for tangible inventions – is somewhat expensive and slow. Patent pending is a more affordable version of a patent, should you really need protection. Copyright protection occurs immediately once something is created in a tangible form, however, there's no legal proof, which is why copyrighting something can be worth the price and process.

Entrepreneurs sometimes ask anyone they talk to about their business idea to sign a confidentiality agreement. This may hinder you. Potential investors and survey participants generally won't do that.

This is partially a function of leverage (who needs whom more). Once you are hiring or collaborating with someone on a deep level where they have access to your innermost workings, asking them to sign an NDA may be appropriate. Use your best judgment. For example, if you are submitting a story, screenplay, or book proposal to a movie production or distribution company, or to potential representation (agent, manager) they won't sign your NDA or confidentiality agreement and may actually ask you to sign something releasing them from any potential liability.

If you are creating something novel to sell, it may fall be worth copyright-ing or patenting, each has different traits.

- IP includes anything original that you create
- IP is protected by U.S. law (laws differ from one country to the next)

- Invention of tangible objects and how they look and function is covered by Patents
- Creation of artistic works is covered by Copyrights

Copyright is the protection given to intangible artistic creations.

- Copyright does not protect ideas, it protects the EXPRESSION of ideas
- Examples include a Script, Movie, Song, Book, Photograph, Software – literary, artistic, educational, or musical form
- Copyright gives the owner the right to make copies and sell them
- Copyright gives its owner the exclusive right to make and exploit (sell or license) copies of a creative work for a limited time
- Copyright length varies from the author's life + 70 years to 120 years if initiated by a corporation
- www.Copyright.gov is where copyright registration and filing occurs, where copyright records appear and more info can be found
- The actual copyright (legal protection) of your work exists the moment you create it, however, that doesn't establish a record of it. The reason you would actually record your copyright with the U.S. copyright office is for proof in case someone steals your IP and you need to establish your ownership
- Symbol is ©
- Costs vary from $65 and up
- Derivative work is a creation based on (derived) something else. Examples include a screenplay based on a book, a podcast based on true events, etc
- "Work for hire" is when a company or hiring party pays a creator to create something. The Hiring Party owns the intellectual property created under that agreement and is considered the author

There are four steps to copyrighting a work. Register yourself, register your work, pay, then upload the work. Note that any information you put on the copyright database becomes a public record.

Prior to uploading any of your own work into the copyright website, it's a good idea to visit and search records, so you are familiar with the database. Search for a copyrighted item, like a song or book, to see how the information is organized.

Copyright Search. You want to see if there is anyone else listed on the copyright record of the song Taylor Swift sang entitled "Our Song." Open an Internet browser to look for that specific song.

- Type Copywright.gov
- Select Other search options, specify title and artist
- Survey results

This is a giant database, so it takes time when you are conducting a wide search (Figures 6.6–6.8).

Patents protect the design and utility of a TANGIBLE creation (jewelry, chair, toothbrush, machine).

- A patent is used to prevent an invention from being created, sold, or used by another party without permission
- You cannot get a patent based on an idea, you need to show how the invention works and is "novel"
- The term of a regular patent (RPA) is 20 years from the date on which the application for the patent was filed in the United States

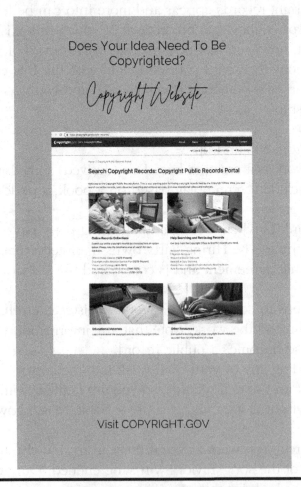

Figure 6.6 Copyright Search Start from US Copyright Website.

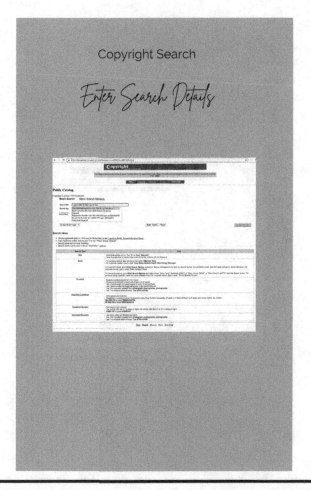

Figure 6.7   Copyright Search Enter Details from US Copyright Website.

- www.USPTO.gov (the United States Patent and Trademark Office) is where patent applications are filed, where records appear, and more info can be found
- Utility patents may be granted to anyone who invents or discovers any new and useful process (how something works)
- Design patents may be granted to anyone who invents a new, original, and ornamental design for an article of manufacture (how something looks)
- Patents are time-consuming to research and apply for and expensive
- Federal law requires the staff at the USPTO to help inventors who apply for a patent without a lawyer
- Symbol is ®

Sometimes inventors file a provisional patent application (PPA) which lasts 1 year. This lets you say you have a "patent pending" status (at www.USPTO.gov)

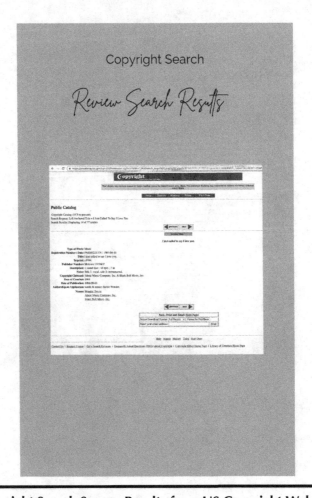

Figure 6.8 Copyright Search Survey Results from US Copyright Website.

for credibility with investors, consumers, vendors, and licensees. Filing a PPA simply allows you to claim "patent pending" status for the invention and is much less work and cost than filing a regular patent. PPA filing fee is under $100.

The steps to patenting your invention include keeping a written record of your work, researching other patents, creating a detailed narrative description of your invention with details of what is novel (new) and drawings, with claims of exactly what will be protected by the patent (Figure 6.9).

There are lawyers who specialize in Intellectual Property, and there are services online which also do this:

■ https://www.legalzoom.com/
■ https://www.nolo.com/

Does Your Idea Need To Be Patented?

USPTO Website

Visit USPTO.GOV

Figure 6.9   USPTO Website by USPTO Website.

Trade secrets of a company may be related to information or processes that aren't clearly patentable or copyrightable. The way to protect them is to use non-disclosure agreements (NDAs). Trade secrets don't need to be registered.

Licensing your intellectual property to others by using an intellectual property license agreement gives you a way to retain ownership of your patent, copyright, or trademark, while you grant someone permission to use some, or all, of your intellectual property rights in a specific way. The licensing agreement would outline the details, fees paid to the owner of the IP, and may be Exclusive, where you grant use only to the other party, or a non-Exclusive License.

Public domain is the designation of a copyright product that is free for everyone to use, generally anything made before 1923. You can check when something was made by searching records at www.COPYRIGHT.GOV.

Creative Commons (CC) licenses are public copyright licenses that enable free distribution, with various restrictions (or none) of an otherwise copyrighted work. The digital world made it very easy to share copyright products and the CC movement sprang up in response to that. CC licenses attempt to balance the idea that possibly there is something more flexible between public domain and copyright. The author decides what the license would be. Descriptions of the concept and licenses can be found at https://creativecommons.org. The U.S. government has nothing to do with these and they confer no legal protection. One reason to use one of the CC licenses is for exposure, to find collaborators and to get your work out there.

Mini Case Study. Ryan McGuire is a creative, artist, and photographer with a discerning eye and an incredible wit. His work runs the gamut from fine art to illustrations, public art, and photography that can be silly, hilarious, bizarre, or random. Generosity and curiosity are hallmarks of his work. In 2011, he founded a website for people in need of pictures, for personal and commercial projects, that they could download and use completely free of charge and without attribution. That generosity has created rabid fans of his work, garnering him loyalty, attention and helping market him. With the ease of digital sharing, this use of the CC0 license (free use with no attribution required) has exposed many people to his work and added to his following. (See the Googly-eyes photo in Chapter 2.) His work and story can be found here: http://mcguiremade.com/.

Record-Keeping/Taxes

Nothing here is tax advice or substitutes for speaking with a tax professional. In your startup endeavors, you are involved in transactions that come with tax consequences, whether you decide to start some corporate structure or delay it until later. Expenses and income of a business are typically reported on a tax return. Keep records consistently. Separate your personal and business income and expenses. When you're ready, add a basic bookkeeping system. In general, the IRS recommends that you should hang on to any documents or evidence of income, deduction, or credit that would be shown on a tax return. In the event that there is any question or audit, you'll have the information should it be required. These may include:

- Bank statements
- Receipts
- Deposit information

- Invoices sent and received
- Canceled checks
- Credit card receipts and statements
- Petty cash slips for small cash payments
- Travel documents for travel expenses

Depending on the type of business you're in, whether you're running it from your home, what and how you deduct, is clearly spelled out on the IRS website. The length of time required to keep the various documentation varies from 3 to 7 years. If you keep all of your records digitally, it's a good idea to back everything up. The rules vary from year to year. Certain types of expenses may be changed on what is allowed; required documentation to prove the expenses may be changed, so it's better to hang on to documents just in case. Certain categories of expenses that are too large, such as travel, meals, and entertainment, might send up a red flag to the IRS, be honest and practical in all of your expenditures. In the event of any question relating to taxes, the burden of proof will be on you to back up every item on your tax return, including supporting documentation.

If you plan to hire workers – whether employees or independent contractors, there is tax-related paperwork that the IRS requires.

In terms of record-keeping, keep the following business documents permanently:

- Tax filings
- Tax returns
- Contracts you've signed (with clients, vendors, contractors, employees, etc.)
- Any Articles of incorporation, should you form a corporation
- Business permits
- Company health, safety, and any other regulatory documents, if applicable
- Annual reports
- Any copyright, patent, trademark, service mark registration, renewals, or related documents
- Current and former banking information, account numbers, passwords, banker name, and contact

Hiring help may incur tax liabilities. The IRS has specific paperwork for this on both sides, hiring party and worker. An employee is different from an independent contractor. If you need cost-effective help as a startup, you are typically hiring an independent contractor to do something specific, in a specific budget and timeline. You don't pay that person's taxes, it's on them. When you hire an employee for regular, ongoing work, you must pay taxes and they must pay taxes on those wages.

To determine whether a person is an employee or an independent contractor, these are some of the factors:

- Does the employer control what the worker does, and how the worker does the job
- Does the employer control the business aspects of the worker's job
- Is there a written contract or benefits
- Will the relationship continue

For tax reporting purposes, the tax form a hiring party gives to an independent contractor to report taxable income, is Form W-9, a Request for Taxpayer Identification Number and Certification. When the contractor fills it out, it captures the information of the person, or company, doing work for your business. From here, you can record their wages. If you pay someone $600 or more, these forms are required by the IRS. Many people on both sides of paying and receiving income ignore the paperwork and rules.

If you have hired an independent contractor, at the end of the year, 1099-NEC (NEC = non-employee compensation) must be filled out by the hiring party and provided to the individual or entity by January 31. This form will report what is paid to the individual or entity and their reporting details (like name, address, SSN, or TIN). All tax payments for that income are up to the contractor. More information about this can be found at the IRS website: https://www.irs.gov/businesses/small-businesses-self-employed/forms-and-associated-taxes-for-independent-contractors.

When you hire employees, the employee fills out the Form W-4, the Employee's Withholding Allowance Certificate, and gives it to the employer. This is how an employer knows how much to tax to withhold throughout the year. The amount withheld will be based on the allowances claimed, more allowances, the lower amount of federal taxes withheld from each paycheck. At the end of the year, employers complete the Form W-2, which reports how much an employer paid an employee, and how much tax is withheld during the year. W-2 must be provided to the employee by January 31.

As your startup grows, consider hiring a bookkeeper or accountant to set up a simple bookkeeping system for you and for occasional tax help. Tax laws change over time. One of the best things about working with a tax professional or CPA is that they stay current with these changes. They can warn you about problems in your return or alert you to tax breaks you may not be aware of.

The various tax forms and paperwork around them can be a bit confusing at first. At this juncture, and when you're setting up an accounting and bookkeeping system, consult with a bookkeeper. Several online companies offer bookkeeping services for a monthly fee, or you may want to ask friends for references. Not every business needs to work with someone monthly, you may find a professional to help you set up your books, and check in at certain intervals, or just get hired to prepare your taxes. Many services will give you a free trial period. Software that freelancers and small businesses use for payroll, taxes, and bookkeeping including:

- https://gusto.com/
- https://bench.co/
- https://www.backoffice.co/
- https://www.remotebooksonline.com/
- https://quickbooks.intuit.com/
- https://www.freshbooks.com/

The Freelancers Union (https://www.freelancersunion.org) is another resource for record-keeping and tax guidance. Others include:

- https://thecreativeindependent.com/guides/a-smart-artists-guide-to-income-taxes/
- https://brasstaxes.com/
- https://www.sunlighttax.com/
- https://www.gyst-ink.com/taxes

In terms of general money management, you have several banking options, and you should compare them before committing. Online-only banks are taking off for small businesses because they have very low fee structures, like Novo.com. Make sure they are protected by the FDIC (it would say on their website). While convenient, and with helpful tech tools, weigh the convenience with the lack of physical branches to deposit cash, and human help. Credit unions offer personal, localized service and are interested in building relationships in a community. Big banks have more ATMs and sometimes a wider breadth of services, however, it's more difficult to build a connection with an actual banker. Fees and deposit requirements are generally higher with mainstream banks.

The beauty of setting up systems, whether social media or analytics dashboards, banking and bookkeeping systems, is that they provide data – the roadmap for progress and movement.

Track and Analyze KPI – The Metrics of Movement

You must be aware of certain data and track it over time in order to understand it. Some information seems self-evident, for example, sales. If you sell 100 more of something every month, then the metrics tell you the business is improving. That's great, however, if you set this up in a way to learn from your movement, then you can make the most of it.

KPI stands for Key Performance Indicators. Once you set numerical goals, such as # of sales I seek to generate per month, # of products to sell, people coming to the website, and so forth, KPIs give you a way to measure these items in relation to your goals. Why set and measure key performance indicators? As a means to understand sales, improve actions and make them more impactful, while eliminating whatever isn't working.

Measuring something numerically will help you learn from it. Quantifying changes, up, down or flat, indicate that something is, or isn't, working. For instance, money generated. Expenses spent. Which products and services are sold and when? Who buys and where did they come from? When you have an online business that incorporates online web traffic, and social media, you can use that information to learn. Here are some of the KPIs you may use:

- Sales
- Web traffic
- Social media engagement
- Successful checkout from your online store
- Incomplete checkout (abandoned carts)
- Amount of time spent on your site
- Where your traffic came from
- Advertising data (clicks)
- Conversion rate (# of shoppers that actually bought)
- Returns
- Average order value (what shopper paid)

The point of KPIs isn't to make more work. The point of defining these is to give you concrete data to find out what's going on. Where are your customers coming from? How many of your customers are buying? What are they buying, and how many items do they buy? Focus on revenue and those activities that directly impact that. You don't need a ton of KPIs, and they should be actionable. They need to show you what improvements you can make to spur sales, signups, subscriptions, referrals, repeat purchases, etc.

Pick one to two key performance indicators at first. Make the process easy, clearly defined, and quantifiable. Look at these in regular intervals, bi-weekly, or monthly. Use Google Analytics and dashboards built into your website (WooCommerce, Shopify, Squarespace, MemberPress, and others). Pick key goals:

- Sales
- Traffic (online sales need traffic)
- Leads
- Time spent on-site
- Abandoned carts

An example would be analyzing sales on a website. If there are few sales, look at traffic. Little to no traffic on your site would translate to even fewer sales. This is a clue about marketing. If people don't know you are selling something, or where to buy it, they won't come to your site and you won't have traffic. Sales in this case require traffic, which requires marketing. Change your marketing to see if your traffic increases, and then your sales.

Other metrics are amounts of gross sales (income prior to deducting any expenses) and net sales (income after expenses). Increasing your profit margin and measuring that is also a great KPI. Here is one example.

Lia is a visual artist. At the end of 2022, she looks ahead to the next year to make some goals for the next year. For 2023, Lia projects that she will earn $30,000 in gross sales of her paintings. As a startup, she plans on spending 30% of that (or $10,000) on her marketing budget. At the end of 2023, say Lia actually made $30,000 in gross sales but spent $15,000 in expenses on marketing and other items.

Her net sales would be $30,000 (gross) – expenses of $15,000 = net sales $15,000.

So Lia actually spent $15,000, 50% of her projected income. What's great is that she hit her target in gross sales. She spent more than she thought, but perhaps that was necessary in order to hit that target. Relevant KPIs to look at would relate to marketing. She should analyze what she spent on different channels (Website, Zoom Events, Google Ads, Social Media) to see if she can figure out which platform brought most of the sales and which didn't perform. Armed with this information Lia can cut or eliminate that expense. An approach for 2024 may be to plan on spending 40–50% of projected gross sales on marketing.

A recommendation would be to boost gross sales targets to $50,000, planning on spending 50% on marketing ($25,000). If she hits those targets, $50,000 – $25,000 would earn her $25,000 in net sales. This example does not focus on repeat versus new clients, however, analyzing that metric could also offer insights into boosting her revenue overall.

Current Clients versus New Clients

For every $1 you spend to reach a current customer, it takes an average of $6 to reach a new customer. New customers are expensive! Therefore, you should take excellent care of your current customers and nurture those relationships. Also, current fans can become your best marketers. Word of mouth from current customers is traditionally the best marketing and you can't buy it, you can only earn it.

Return on Investment (ROI) is a way to figure out the benefit of a particular expense. By using the previous example of $1 spent to secure a current customer's purchase versus $6 spent to attract a new customer, ROI for current customers is much better. Even though you might want to focus on your current customers, you need to spend time on both. Here's an example.

$$ROI = (TOTAL\ REVENUE - TOTAL\ COST)/TOTAL\ COST$$

Example: Lia spends $150 boosting posts on Facebook. As a result she sells two works totaling $250 in income. So, Lia's ROI for those boosted posts is
$250 minus $150,
divided by $150
= 0.66 (expressed as a percent is 66%)

$$ROI = (TOTAL\ REVENUE - TOTAL\ COST)/TOTAL\ COST$$

- (250 – 150)/150
- 100/150
- = 0.66 – in other words, 66%

■ That means for every $1 Lia spent on advertising using boosted posts on Facebook, she grossed $1.66 and netted 66 cents.

These data are valuable. Lia now has an idea of the effectiveness of the Facebook boosted posts. These data grow even more valuable when compared to what happened on Instagram with the same budget. The results from her spending on IG was only a little bit higher (70%), but she sold 12 smaller pieces, all of which had a pop-art, whimsical sensibility. The data indicate that she reached twice as many people, all of which were in a younger demographic. This tells Lia that her impact with the Instagram audience could have more potential if she only marketed a certain kind of work on that platform. Her next advertising campaign will focus on Instagram, targeting younger buyers.

Cultivate Community for Motivation

Creators walk a thin line between activities that require us to be an introvert or extrovert. We need to be both at times, alternating when necessary. Many of us require solitude to actually make anything, but then we need feedback to understand the impact of our creation. It's important to be more extroverted to share, sell, and promote our offerings.

Not everyone is comfortable at each phase, and we need support. Sometimes creating can make us feel isolated and lonely. We also need support due to the ups and downs of the creative field, from PLUs (people like us). It is a good idea to join the right group for connection along the way. First, decide what you need from an organization. Search by discipline and industry, broad or narrow. You can search by:

■ Region or geography
■ Ethnicity, age, gender
■ Product/service focus
■ Industry or sector
■ Ethos and spirit, mission
■ Founders

Make sure there are opportunities to connect with others, then make the effort. Seek out a group with people on varying levels. You want to stretch and also to help others along the way. Look online and ask friends. Eventbrite, trade organizations, social media, or platforms like Twitch, Clubhouse, Meetup, Craigslist, or Discord.

If you don't find one, start it yourself.

Note that a non-profit organization (which usually uses a web domain ending with .edu or .org) will often have a different agenda than one that is for-profit. Make sure that the activities and meetings of the organization, whether online or in-person, suit your personality. To make the most of your group, add events to your calendar. Make time to interact with the community. As with so many things in life, you get what you put into it. Keep looking around, just zooming with a bunch of cool like-minded people all doing their best and trying – can be very inspirational! (Figure 6.10).

Channeling your skills and talents into a startup is a worthy use of your time, gifts, and talents. By guiding your entrepreneurial spirit into launching an MVP into the world, you create a direct route of your creativity to commerce. Productivity into profits and freedom. While the path can be challenging, keep perspective and humor, and include all of your many talents into the process. You can do this, and the world needs your vision and unique abilities. Now, more than ever.

Thank you for sharing this journey with me. Please stay in touch!

Figure 6.10   Quote by Paula Landry.

Index

Note: Page numbers followed by f and t indicate figures and tables respectively.

Printed in the United States
by Baker & Taylor Publisher Services

Printed in the United States
by Baker & Taylor Publisher Services